TELEPATHY, LOVE, AND
THE RESCUE OF TRUTH

TELEPATHY, LOVE *and* the RESCUE *of* TRUTH

BECOMING LUCID WITHIN THE COLLECTIVE DREAM

SUSAN L. GURAN

Epigraph Books
Rhinebeck, New York

Telepathy, Love, and the Rescue of Truth: Becoming Lucid Within the Collective Dream © Copyright 2026 by Susan L. Guran

All rights reserved. No part of this book may be used or reproduced in any manner without the consent of the author, except in critical articles or reviews. Contact the publisher for information.

Paperback ISBN 9781966293330

Library of Congress Control Number 2026901400

Cover art by Susan L. Guran
Book and cover design by Colin Rolfe

Epigraph Books
22 East Market Street, Suite 304
Rhinebeck, New York 12572
(845) 876-4861
epigraphpublishing.com

To my children and clients who graciously opened themselves up to new possibilities without fear or hesitation, providing the learning scape by which this book could come into form.

To the seekers who know there is more to reality than what can be measured.

CONTENTS

Introduction	xi
Opening: *Blueprints of Freedom*	xvii

PART I
SEPARATION
The Layers of Noise That Lead Us Away

- **This World and the Other One** — 3
  What Is Real and What Is Not
- **Mind vs. Imagination** — 7
  Walking Through Walls
- **Identity vs. Integrity** — 12
  Living Beyond the Self
- **Good As Gold** — 26
  The Veil of Virtue
- **Temptation** — 29
  The Seduction of Earthly Desire

PART II
REMEMBRANCE
Returning to Union

- **Confusion of Realms** — 39
  The Astral and The Ethereal
- **The One and The Many** — 45
  Why and How Telepathy Occurs

- **Sacred Architecture**   51
  The Living Temple
- **Faith and Trust**   58
  New Lines of Sight
- **Blurred Altars**   61
  The Quest for Enlightenment
- **Love and Truth**   67
  There's No Place Like Home

Closing: *Road to Recovery*   75

PART III
THE METHODS
Tools for Transformation

The Methods	80
Resources to support embodiment	101
Charts	102

TELEPATHY, LOVE, AND THE RESCUE OF TRUTH

IT'S TIME TO REMEMBER

*Before you came tumbling into the glaring light
you set forth your desires as the path that you would follow
and left tiny beacons along the way.
You agreed to ride your imagination for the becoming of you.
But someone must have told you not to be a dreamer
and you believed them
because you forgot that dreaming and imagination are your guides, set upon your desires.*

*These are not the desires that grunt and grind and steal – NO
these are the desires that expand your heart
and have you reaching for the clouds on a steed of light.*

*Those dreams you dream,
however grand they seem,
they inform your destiny.
Snip the ties that hold them back.
Feel the wings fluttering in your heart.
Breathe and set your feet upon the path.
Release the fear that clouds your eyes
so you can see the flecks of luck and love that you have set before yourself.*

*Breathe and catch the sparkles with your mind.
Follow your fascination.
Thank the stars for heading you off, again and again,
at every oblivious turn.*

INTRODUCTION

Why This Book Exists and Why This Matters

I'm writing this book to help relieve unnecessary suffering by bringing awareness to how we can participate in the interconnectedness of all things. My goal is to lead others away from anxiety and confusion and back to their psychic and telepathic nature, not only to experience what Love truly is and where it is found, but also to understand how, together, we can create a new reality.

In these pages, I present the structure of the default reality—the one we didn't make or choose—to uncouple it from the **true** reality and illustrate what obscures this. When we understand the arrangement of what is in and around us, we can remember what is available to us and where it can be found. We can remove the barriers that allow us to discern what is false or true and recall why we must give up one world to experience the other.

I am sharing *from my own point of discovery* information that emerged experientially to offer a guide for effecting change and a template for sorting through the distortions that have been handed down to us. The deeper reality has a direct effect on the physical and we not only ***can*** participate in this, but we must. We are all capable of understanding what it is, where it is and how to converse with it because it is our original home and language. I will present an interpretation of this structure that has practical value and application.

I came upon these discoveries through the evolution of my work, which lead me to communicating with and treating animals *telepathically* with homeopathic medicine. Much of what I learned was "accidental" in the sense that I was following where I was being led to and discovering things I did not know were possible. This trajectory was seeded by a suggestion by one of my teachers in homeopathy school that remedies could potentially be administered by writing them down on a piece of paper or just by saying their name. This idea so fascinated me, that I set to work in testing it on my own children throughout their childhoods. We all benefited immensely from this long-term experiment, and I learned a lot from them because they could feel the remedies as they received them and would tell me if I had given them the wrong one. During that time, I was still determining remedies conventionally using rubrics in a computer program to narrow down choices, rather than working intuitively to find the exact match.

Ultimately, my endeavors and explorations taught me how to consistently tap into a place, a feeling, a state of being, that greatly enhances well-being and brings about a deep sense of peace. My work takes place in the transitional state between waking and sleeping, referred to as the hypnogogic state.[1] When I

---

[1] *refer to the practice* "Hypnogogic Suspension" *in* **Part III: The Method**

learned to suspend myself here for extended periods, I discovered that it was a gateway to a realm of pure Love. Engaging in telepathic meeting points lead to the discovery that these encounters bring about feelings of **Bliss!** This is because this is something we are meant to be doing. It is in our nature to communicate this way.

Years of corroboration from clients regarding the information conveyed by their animals and the healing that was set in motion via the remedies that were sent to them, repeatedly highlighted an insight that I could not ignore—*information that **alters physical reality** can be sent and received via the ethereal imaginal thought space*. The world we know is not set up to explain this, yet the effects can be experienced and observed.

Things happen that we can't explain because our model of reality is flawed. Therefore, a new vantage point is needed. As long as we are conditioned to participate from a limited range of perception, we will feel unsettled. It is because information is missing from our common understanding of reality that so many people feel lost and confused. I have also felt lost and confused for much of my life! And I wasn't always in tune with telepathic and clairvoyant abilities. Though I trusted my intuition in many situations, I also overrode it more often than not and experienced the harm that comes from not paying attention.

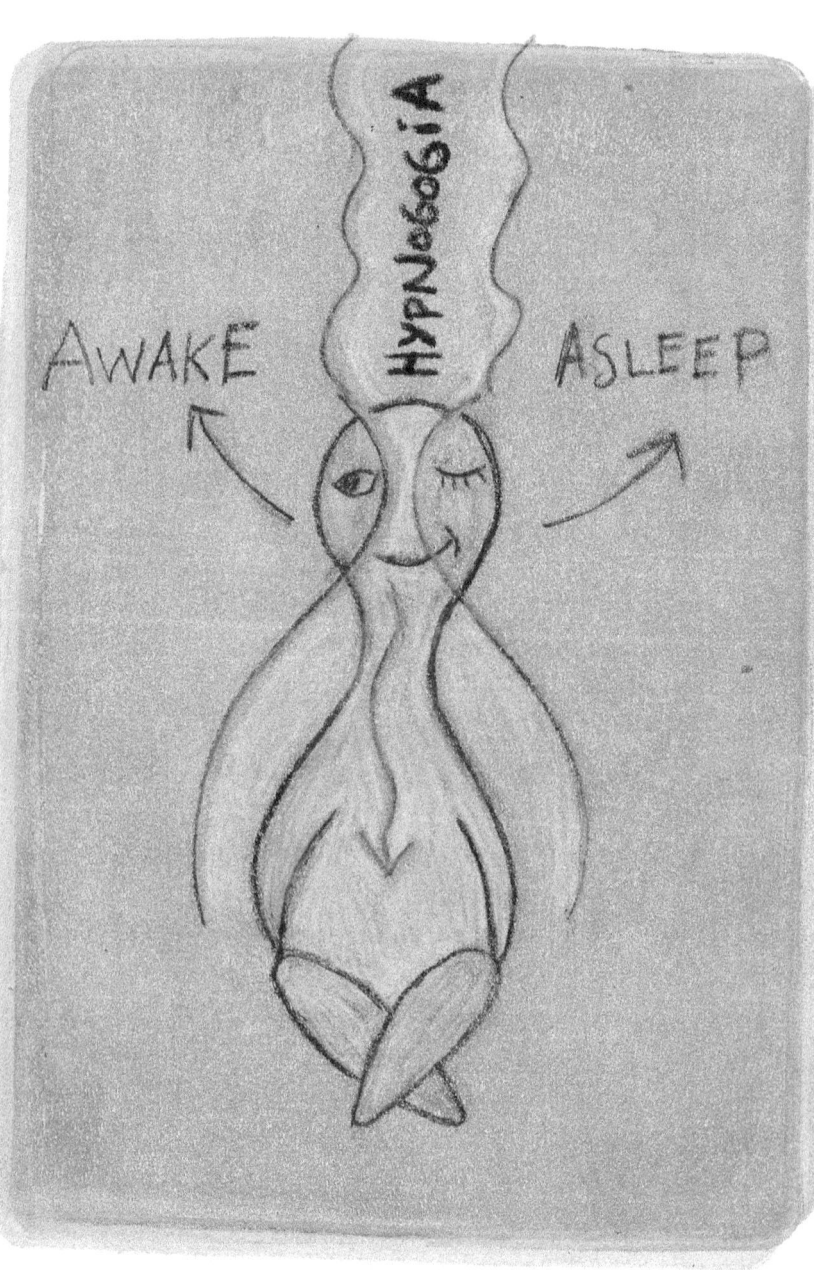

What Telepathy Means and Why It's Important

Telepathy is the innate ability to send and receive information to and from other points of consciousness. It is an expansion into limitless reality that holds the key to returning to our original state of being and reshaping the outer world. Our directed focus illuminates the metamorphic space where a vision, feeling, sensation or inspiration conveys information beyond words. Such transmissions are a multi-sensory display where many things occur at once to convey information that sparks transformation. When we reclaim this ability, we come to understand how we can create the world we desire.

All animals are telepathic and so are we.[2] When you think of someone and they contact you shortly afterwards, it is your sensorial experience of their energy, form and presence that brings about this common telepathic occurrence that enlivens the pathway between two points of consciousness.[3]

This book is not about mind reading, it is about re-entering the truth that *we were never disconnected*. You don't need to be "special" to feel this. You only need to see what is standing in your way and learn how to navigate beyond it. Before we can remember each other, we need to forget what divided us. By releasing what is <u>not</u> true, we can return to union.

This is an offering of recognition. It won't feel

---

[2] *refer to the practice* "Inviting Presence" *in* **Part III: The Method**

[3] *refer to the practice* "Engaging in Conversation" *in* **Part III: The Method**

like I'm telling you something new. It will feel like a reminder of something you already know. It is a navigational tool for coming back to where we sense one another without interference. If you're here, it's because your soul remembers how this leads us to a Love beyond fear.

OPENING
Blueprints of Freedom

There is an inner world that is vast and accessible. It is not *your* inner world, it is <u>the</u> inner world, as tangible and necessary to our collective well-being as the outer world. It is the foundation of the world we create outside of ourselves. This province, hidden in plain sight, seeks to confer with us. Everything in it is alive and interactive. If we learn how to engage with it, we will not need to quest after the elusive goal of enlightenment, though we will become enlightened!

Consciousness awaits our telepathic reunion with Love and Truth, by which we become *the collective causal event* that revises physical reality and the trajectory of mankind. Each one of us has a part to play in this. True reality requires us to have a hand in creation. While all of life is designed to evolve in response to changes in the environment, we have the power to change the environment and affect evolution itself.

Most of us know in our hearts that a world of Love exists, but from the one we have inherited, it is difficult to imagine. Centuries of participation in a world divorced from abiding Love have created the frightening display we now see, where Truth is blended with lies. The unremitting pandemonium that surrounds us leaves us confused about where and how to find authentic Love, *even though it is accessible to each and every one of us.*

This world appears to be full of things we want, yet a sense of satisfaction and contentment rarely penetrates our hearts. We know that information is missing because we can't find our way to peace. *How can we create a new world if we accept this one as something we must adapt to?* We need to see the false construct exactly as it is so that we can cast it away. We need to become lucid to end the nightmare. *Are we lucid or are we letting the dream happen to us?* The nightmare shows us what occurs when we lose track of Love, which is both a place and a state of being. There is a perennial passageway we can go to that will lead us there.

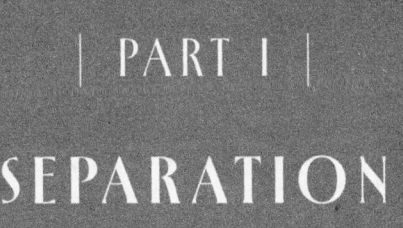

| PART I |

SEPARATION

*The Layers of
Noise that Lead
Us Away*

THIS WORLD AND THE OTHER ONE
What Is Real, What Is Not

Looking upon the natural world, we can see that things are in order. The sun rises every day, the trees and plants cleanse our air and feed us, and there is an abundance of beauty in the landscape to feed our souls. Overlaid upon this is manmade conceptual reality, which darkens our view of the world and ourselves, and separates human beings out as "not a part of"—a blight upon the earth. It is a world full of negativity and violence that creates fear and unhappiness and occludes our ability to relate to a more hopeful and benevolent world.

Our shared anxiety is rooted in a paradigm that has been handed down to us throughout the ages. From this legacy, we play out roles of dominance and submission, where much of our energy is spent on protecting ourselves from the destructive potential *of our own kind*—protecting our lives, our viewpoints, our livelihoods, our stuff. Every story of strength and power is distorted to become power OVER, to objectify, manipulate and exploit. We can't recognize human need in a system of reward and punishment. We can't learn and grow in this system.

Manmade reality is *inhospitable* and for this reason, many of us feel like outsiders. The conclusion drawn is that *there is something wrong with me.* Rarely does it occur to us that the environment we are in is a misconception. We can forgive ourselves for upholding this dubious inheritance because we didn't know better. We have tried our best to live within it. Now it's time for something new. There is no place to go, because we are already there. We only need to see it.

There are two worlds. The *Real* World and the *False* World, the world of nature or the SUPERnatural and the world of delusion. What we currently perceive to be our reality is an <u>altered</u> state. Our participation keeps it alive. It is held together mentally. Analytical thinking and borrowed ideas suffuse the imaginal space with ruminations that obstruct our ability to experience clairsentience.

The false world is like slime. It has no structure. What is false places itself on the platform of truth, becoming half-truth, not for the purpose of disclosure, but to exist. It lives a parasitic life. Demons are the symbolic embodiment of parasitic energy that feeds on that which is weakened. We are weakened by abuse and violence of thought and deed, which pushes us deeper into the delusional reality so that we become invested in moving against life.

The world we see is made of pieces and parts with nothing to tie them together. The "system" is not functional because it is unnatural. Therefore, it is not self-sustaining without the sacrifice of what is real. We can't find what is real if we are not aware of where realness resides. We are not lost, we are deceived. There is a war going on—in our bodies, in our countries, in our minds. It is a story of inherent wrongness.

In the <u>altered</u> reality, social acceptance is based on similar ways of positioning rather than allied visions that move us toward the welfare of the whole. The *persona* we don separates us from our trustworthiness and fuels a longing for re-union. In this false world, we are instructed to focus on the individual journey.

To come into collective harmony, we must shed the delusion. To say that we are deluded is not to say that the interplay we see before us does not exist. To change our world as it is today, we do not renounce the physical and call it an illusion, we renounce the mental/emotional framework that misinforms us and make a commitment to what <u>rightly</u> informs the material world.

Unconscious, reactionary patterns are developed when we believe we are a part of the <u>altered</u> reality. These patterns serve our emotional survival in a seemingly malefic world. To see what is, is to end our participation. The world that crumbles is the world that doesn't exist.

Pure perception occurs in the **un**altered world that recognizes our rapport with natural forces that are in support of our evolutionary growth. We reclaim the original essence by reinstating our loyalty to this territory. In the **un**altered world, we each represent a unique aspect of consciousness viewing the world through an unparalleled perspective, a vision that is accessible only from one's own inimitable vantage point. From here, we can apply our vision toward what we **en**vision to bring it into being.

The inner realm has practical value in helping us build the world we want, a world where we belong. When we engage "out there" from *within*, we come into a state of coherence to revise physical reality. The outer reality is reformed through our inquiries and directives, but if we are absent from this role, we are left with the *default reality*, which disembodies us and gives rise to mayhem and evil acts.

In the paradigm that reflects Truth—the **un**altered world—each moment is met in the spirit of union and collaboration. All challenges arise in a state of mutual reception. A self-governing community emerges through support of personal strength, desire and initiative and each being's unique function within the whole, where all qualities that support the health of a community can blossom. Without this transcendent nourishment, we devour one another.

- (False Power) FORCE <u>demands</u> service through submission
- (Natural Power) LOVE <u>elicits</u> service through support

MIND VS. IMAGINATION
Walking Through Walls

Manipulation of reality occurs through captivation of the imagination. The imagination can be used to connect us or to frighten us, to terrorize or create. When we're frightened, we can't use it as what it was meant for—a doorway to a supreme consciousness, of which we are a part. This is how the false world controls and enslaves.

The repository we call the "mind" is tenaciously occupied with habitual thought patterns that separate us from what is real. *What can we see when we are blinded by our own thoughts?* Only our own thoughts. The unfastened awareness of the preoccupied mind detaches us from the wholeness of the vessel. By identifying with it, we are disembodied and the vacated vessel is then susceptible to occupation by other forces.

The churning of the disembodied thought space creates habits of living and perceiving that place a veneer upon pure perception and expression. Harm is caused by our **reactions** to manipulated perception. This is the delusion that oppresses and has us working against what is natural.

We uphold the delusion because we can't receive something that we don't know exists. We can't call on faith to carry us across the bridge if we don't trust that there is something on the other side. We join with power when the separation no longer blocks our vision. Pure perception is an active and communal way station for the restructuring of the material. When unwrangled thoughts recede, the channel reception clears.

We are continuously attacked both out there and "in here" because our minds are conditioned for attack and being attacked. The imagination is drawn outward toward the specters of a false world that is orchestrated to elevate fear. All that we submit to out of fear welcomes the unholy. The distracted mind acts as a shield or veil, separating us from the free-flowing energy of Love. *How can we differentiate hijacked perceptions from transmissions that arise from the underlying reality?*

Imagination has a critically important role to play in our participation with the unseen. It is undermined by manufactured thought that we assume to be our own. Our disorderly attention stretches and reaches and grasps for external validation, tipping us here or there, creating imbalances and making us weak. All the while other aspects of consciousness await our commitment. The limited compositions of the mind are used to decipher what makes us good or bad, lovable or unlovable, worthy or unworthy. While we are busy searching for approval and self-definition, the opportunity for profound otherworldly exchange is calling for our return.

The "mind" ruminates on what is known, occupying the potential clearing with mental tournaments and overtaking the vessel of creation that

informs and guides us. Our misleading impressions obscure the communications we could be receiving. There is a place deeper than the mind that involves thought that travels through the conduit of sensing/feeling/knowing. It is a cosmic meeting place.

Being directed from "out there" intercepts the imaginal system which is designed to receive and transmit. Beneath this interception is power, integration, wholeness. Through our separation from the fullness of the imaginal realm, we disconnect from the faculty of psychic vision.

To find relief from our thoughts, we must form a window to another world where the rules are different than we were told. Its existence endures through our living and breathing essence, murderer or saint. The light shines clearly and directly on what has always been. Permission to enter is granted by way of our allegiance.

Language shapes our perception of what is real or possible, yet the world of words can bar our way to direct experience. Words are the weapon used to create a false reality through exploitation of the imagination, affecting our moods and motivations and divorcing us from the unified power that amends physical reality. Our collective delusion turns words into tools of persuasion, such that the aim of communication—to unite—is lost.

There are no man-made laws or rules that can rein in the chaos as long as we are unaware of how it originates. In Truth, life is simple. Complexity is the byproduct of over conceptualization. Collectively, the chaos is ramped up to an unbearable level but is a reflection of the inner chaos and confusion of the limited, outwardly focused mind. Therefore, Truth is obscured for all. When the inner chaos clears, the outer chaos falls away. This resolution affects the world and those around us.

There is a direct outer experience and there is a direct inner experience and together they constitute the true reality. Everything that stands in the way of this is *conditioning*. Without conditioned thought we would be able to collaborate harmoniously and set the world on fire with miracles

It is our task to extend life through a consortium, carving a path for the unimpeded life force through imaginal insight. Our inspired fantasies are the path. Soul fulfillment is complete. As prisoners of thought we hold the key to liberation.

Home base is found just below the surface of ordinary thought. The empty space that broadcasts and receives is free of the rebound effect of reflection and projection. It is the level of reality by which the human being is poised to sustain a world of harmonious design, orchestrated by LOVE. Every animal is wired to claim this space. Every plant. All of nature. But only human beings are the inventors of worlds.

> All is in motion, moving to become, never to be repeated. Individual life expresses itself to sustain the whole. The whole is contained within the part, the part is held within the whole. Human consciousness can choose what it will be.

IDENTITY VS. INTEGRITY
Living Beyond the Self

Captivating the imagination alone does not support a false reality. The other component is the artificial self. This identity, or "overself," is the false God we worship. It is the attachment entity that dethrones the inner sun.[1]

The "I" project displaces communication and collaboration that occurs via the inner cosmos. It travels alone, experiencing itself as singular and separate and is given visions to pursue that do not relieve the terror of living a life without transcendent meaning. The past gets brought to the present as we rehearse patterns, habits and viewpoints that seem to bring comfort. But in the present, they have the value of old smelly socks.

We are well supported in the construction of a self. We begin with nothing and learn to fashion the appearance of "trade value." A well-constructed self seems like a reasonable mode of exchange. Our survival feels threatened if we can't find the right formula, yet every iteration, no matter how glamorous, fails us. The mask we don allows us to participate in a world

---

[1] *refer to the practice* "Igniting The Inner Sun" *in* **Part III: The Method**

of deception without feeling consciously disturbed. But this being is merely a chalk figure which cannot earnestly collaborate. As soon as we erase it, we recognize our role within the living kaleidoscope of life to see that we are not the only bead spinning, dropping, sparkling across the rolling terrain.

The carefully crafted persona is our protection from the peer group on which we depend. It is both our safety and our straitjacket. Our healthy development is a threat to a precarious system; therefore, we are accepted into the false world at great sacrifice to our nature. We become skillful at diluting our sincerity as a matter of survival. Acceptance is inevitably tentative, available to those who cooperate with certain beliefs, or pretend to. Our habit is to either appear harmless or to oversell ourselves. False humility keeps us safe by reducing our threat to others.

Our image of self is presented as an unspoken message that tells one group, *"I'm like you—don't shoot."* But simultaneously, tells another, *"I'm the enemy,"* resulting in continuous anxiety. We are safe in the fold and sitting duck at once. Without true power, we must either devitalize ourselves or overpower one another to get what we want or need. When we participate in the unbalancing of others we thwart/weaken/diminish the flow of Love/Power/Truth within, among and between. Because of this false way of seeing, what we need is not accessible.

What gets in the way of developing self-awareness is our identification with beliefs and ideologies that occupy our awareness, tying it up in the embellishment of a self that is quite literally another entity that occupies

IDENTITY VS. INTEGRITY

the space we have forsaken. This identity displaces the true self, shunting it off to the background.

We can come back to our true nature because it is where we began. This world is SAFE because there has been a misunderstanding about what and where reality is. The fundamental reality and the fundamental self are the same. The byproduct of self-awareness is tuning in to the stirrings of the unseen. We develop vision. We can see. We are the seer. Then we can know what we are here for.

Our kingdom of origin is a place where sameness is NOT what binds us. Our place within it arises from the functionality of the Vision. The Vision is dynamic and inviting and requires our conscious participation. We want to be seen, but really it is our vision that must be seen and presented to the world, not the self. To "see myself as" is to point

> What if your life is a work of art and has nothing to do with becoming someone or proving your worth? What if you don't need to sell yourself? What if getting yourself together or feeling like you know what you're doing has no meaning in the grand scheme? What if life isn't a race or a series of successes and failures? What if it isn't rushing you, judging you and casting shadows upon your heart? What if life is an endless opportunity for expression, reception, interconnectedness, transformation, revelation? What if you are a lustrous crystal, spinning, dropping and reflecting the light inside a giant kaleidoscope, imprinting a radiant pattern upon the "has been and will be" of evolution?

our vision in the wrong direction. When we become visionary, we can stop the game of building a self.

Unification/bliss is fleeting and incomplete unless we abandon the false vista. The delusional personality forms the basis of the delusional default reality. To dismantle that reality, we need to break through the bedrock of the false self. When we give up the management of the image, we free ourselves to sense and feel directly. Sensing/feeling is vision from within. INsight.

A community that aligns with Truth is not afraid to explore, discuss and contemplate perspectives. The group is securely connected because it is not dependent on similarity of viewpoints. It exists to build, create, support, and sustain the whole. The nurturing of the individual contributes to the health of the whole and the health of the whole allows us to engage in a vision that encompasses love, beauty, and joy. We are each an integral piece.

In the false reality, we are worthy if we can prove our worthiness, most often at the expense of another. The need to prove our worth permeates all that we do, barring access to free-flowing telepathic exchange.

Conditional worthiness makes us conditionally merciful, which is at the root of our unease. Sensing that I and my brothers and sisters may not offer mercy to one another means we are all in danger. Atheism and our reverent devotion to "science" have accelerated the death of mercy because without transcendence of the mundane it is easy to believe in unworthiness. We can use our will to walk away from fear, restoring our

IDENTITY VS. INTEGRITY

merciful nature, but only if we know where Love is. Our "free" will is only free if Love is within reach.

Coaches tell us to work harder, work smarter, show this part, that part, create a new piece and present it just so, "become the best you can be." Yet this isn't the advice we need. We need to be directed to the exit. Our masks of protection harm us by keeping us separated from our essential nourishment. To dismantle the confusion of the default reality, we need to dismantle the false self. Separation from Love is the delusion. If we are on a solo journey, we are not operating from reality. The feeling of separation is about *not seeing that it doesn't exist!* The ego is a word to describe the separator.

Our guardedness is not without reason. Guilt, shame and group pressure, subtle or overt, mean Love is not on offer. Some people run, some hide, some turn and fight. None of these strategies are solutions. To find Truth, we must disentangle ourselves from the deluded group.

The more we define ourselves, the further away we move from Truth. As long as we are disconnected from Truth, we will be fundamentally merciless. As we place one mask upon another to refine and enhance our performance, we may be afforded accolades, but our status is eternally in jeopardy, stimulating us to envy—a sense of threat that we may lose our place by the perceived greater worthiness of another. When we feel (falsely) worthy because we have won a prize or so, pride leaves us vulnerable to manipulation and sets us apart, when what we really need and want is to come together.

> I am a condition that is ever-changing, a state of evolution that never solidifies.

The identity gathers labels and fixed qualities upon which to sustain itself, molded by a past, a personality and hopes and wishes for the future. The fabricated predictability of man-made environments tricks us into believing in the fictitious borders and boundaries of the static self out of which the feeling of division brings us to despair. Visionary stagnation results from holding an <u>image</u> of self when we are an integral aspect of the ever-changing flow of life. Inner sight brings us to the understanding that our reflection is not who we are. *Why would we fall in love with our reflection when we have found Love?*

ALL things are ever-changing. The strength and power of a wild animal does not emerge from the comfort of its sense of being-ness, but from its responsiveness to the moment. It is adaptation that draws out our strength and resourcefulness and teaches us to study our *environment* so as to understand and harmonize with it. *But what is our true environment?*

Identity interferes with our ability to recognize our essential nature and our adaptability. We are changing and evolving from moment to moment. In our artificially crafted world, this is imperceptible, as we engage in building fortresses against unpredictability. To return to our nature requires a shedding of the outer definitions of who we are. Some we chose, some were acquired by default, some were slapped upon us without our permission.

The fulfillment sought by the "overself" involves setting oneself apart as special, which creates the illusion that we are isolated. The pursuit of specialness vandalizes our potential for partnership, co-creation, community, harmony and is one of the most destructive features of human relations. Every conflict is an effort to set ourselves apart. To be "right," the other must be wrong. To be worthy, I must compare myself to someone who is *unworthy* or *less worthy*. We have something much grander to create than this.

What makes us untrustworthy is our primary loyalty to the image of self built around perceived "earnings." Specialness sets us up for comparison where there can only be inferior or superior. No unity. No oneness. As we seek to become greater than, we feel lesser than. The need to "stand apart" alienates and deceives us. As something greater or lesser, we can't proceed with the function that surrounds our immortal destiny. The great deeds or qualities of others are a threat to our need to be admired, to be "outstanding." We must examine the form in which these ambitions appear so we can let them go to prepare for unification.

Favoritism is a means of control by those in authority, including parents, teachers, bosses, etc. Even though it may seem to make us feel good to be the "favorite," it is a tenuous experience at best. It creates a sense of dependency in those who are favored and they will fight to maintain their status, either covertly or overtly. This undermines the structure of families and communities.

At the root of our divisiveness is a system where people scramble over one another to maintain their status so that we are blinded to the beautiful qualities in others and even threatened by those qualities. This creates opposition even among lovers, friends, and siblings who are stimulated by the past hurts of the many forms of favoritism that occur within families where one or the other was either bypassed or upheld as the chosen or golden one.

When we are put on a pedestal, we secretly cringe because we know we will fall off or be pushed off sooner or later. It never feels deserved because *it is not real.* We learn that allowing this aggrandizement permits us to feel worthy and affords us special treatment. *What do we sacrifice to maintain this status? In how many ways will we subvert ourselves to grab the prize?*

All forms of favoritism keep us deeply rooted in an unhealthy, divisive system. When we are set apart to feel (falsely) powerful, we participate in Evil. When we move away from this, we are met with a world of infinite possibility that is ready to uphold the union of the seen and unseen. In channeling our collective power, we are authentically powerful.

Getting to the nitty-gritty is getting to the one true self that is not a self at all. When we take ourselves back to nothing we find that nothing is everything. As nothing we can receive something. We are not a musician until we are the music. We can feel when we hit that note, but it's not the only note. It allows for others to hit their notes and it's a part of a larger composition, not something that sets us apart or makes us great, but something for which we may feel appreciated, and for which we can appreciate ourselves. No fanfare. Just thankfulness.

We all have a function that is bigger than we are conditioned to accept. Grandeur vs. grandiosity. To recognize and fulfill the grandeur is to employ our interconnectedness, putting together the pieces that allow Love, Beauty and Truth to guide and inform our interactions. There is no creation without collaboration. When we believe in the false self, we starve the soul. When the individual life sees that it does not exist, unification becomes apparent.

The self-focused life feels void of meaning, which is why we can attain all that we think we desire and still feel empty and alone. Our identity is a boundary that obscures our boundlessness. But each "free" human is a doorway to the true reality. In partnership to the whole, we are fortified. There is nothing to deplete.

What we really want is The Grand Feeling. A feeling that has not been defined, but which we have tasted before. It is the feeling that comes from fulfilling one's true function, one's destiny, from a vista that cannot be seen from anywhere else but our unique vantage point. Our real destiny is driven by passion towards something that magnetizes, something we are fascinated by and drawn to *and not alone in creating!* Whatever that is, we are meant to explore it, know it, integrate it, share it. Each one of us represents a unique panorama from which to engage and bring forth beauty and structure.

The identity in which we take pride, that we hold dear, is easily threatened with annihilation through whatever we identify with. And hence, demonic behavior overtakes our nature. Compassion and mercy are buried beneath this state, so we learn to feign

IDENTITY VS. INTEGRITY

compassion. Sincerity is inaccessible because we are continuously under threat of being dismantled in what we take to be ourselves and discovered as an imposter. Proof that the "I" is fiction is that we can observe it. The "observer" is the true being.

The "I" is a member of the unmerciful clan. It will never Love you. When you feel mercy and compassion for others—ALL others—you will know that you have resigned the false self.

Love and Truth go together, so when we are in contact with Love, we can't ignore Truth. Uniting with Love erases our sense of separateness. The embodiment of separateness is the "self". The embodiment of Love is unity. **Love** oversees the cohesive functioning of the whole.

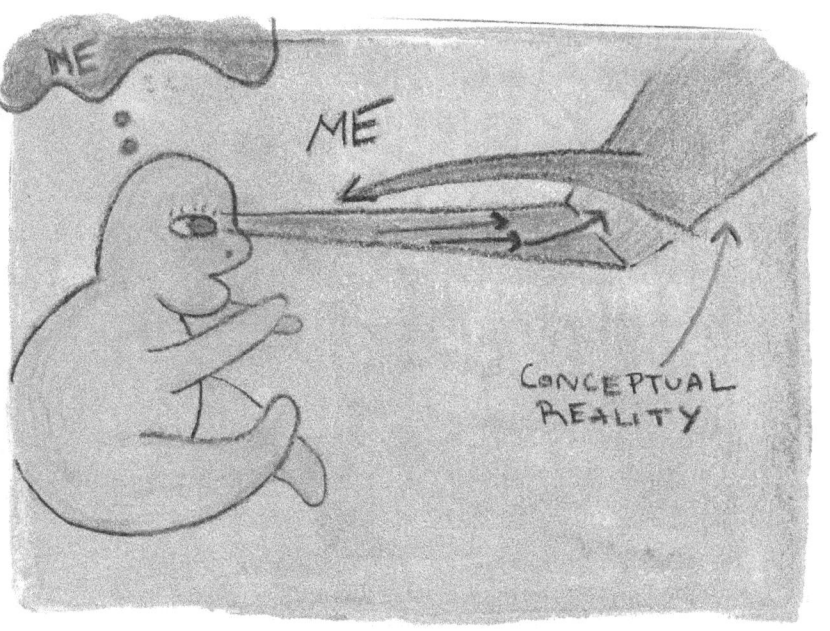

Consciousness is made of vantage points. We are not higher or lower than anything. Panning back from the minutiae of the self (concept) allows for a view of the bigger picture through which we can serve.

Love is within us and we are within Love. Instead of seeing life through a mirror, Love allows us to see it as it is.

We experience our essential desires when we are in contact with reality. We are in contact with reality when we remove and bury the dead monkey on our back, the false garb. Then we can see that reality, which contains our destiny, is both unfolding and creating itself. If we are in contact with it, our effect on others is to bring them into contact with reality as well. This is authenticity. First we establish the relationship, then we allow it to guide and nourish us.

The person we miss the most is the one who lies beneath the illusory self. The one who is magnificent and merciful. When we find him/her, we will see that our task is to raze the system.

Man's greatest fear in knowing himself is that he will discover that he is bad and wrong. But self-awareness will only show him what he **believes** about himself. The reflection we are avoiding is the reflection of our beliefs, not our unique aspect of being. *Do you want to notice what you believe so you can fling it to the wind?*

We have a unified mission to impress Love upon the material world. Human consciousness transcends that of an earthworm for the very reason that we are here to create worlds of infinite beauty. This is the raison d'être for all of humanity. We can't get out of our collective quagmire unless we understand how the seen and unseen worlds are structured and how they interact. This is how we can actively and consciously guide and be guided by the unfolding of creation. Central to this mission is the deliberate and conscious dissolution of self that paves the way for us to merge with the fire of the inner sun and direct the power that burns away the deception standing in our way.

GOOD AS GOLD
The Veil of Virtue

Good and Evil and Love and Hate are separate from eternal Love. Equating Love with goodness sets us up for the impossible task of falling always on the side of good, where we must continuously earn our right to exist. Scoring and keeping score is the method by which we accumulate goodness. Good does not equate to Love because "good" is defined by the ideational tinkerings of man. Goodness is subjective and outwardly determined. Our accumulated goodness can topple at any moment. As soon as the accolades end, we are looking over our shoulder. If we are trying to be a good person, we cannot be authentic and true. Wanting to be <u>seen</u> as "good" cuts us off from Love *and leads to evil acts.*

Goodness and badness are ever-changing and unreliable determinants of right and wrong. The *right* thing arises from the internal compass. Our intrinsic nature does not need to take direction from beliefs or moral codes. Sincere, humble, integrated, pure are not the same as good. These are unearthed through contact with wholeness. The "good" thing is about standing in line for praise over punishment. The guiding flame within is the authentic justice system, flawlessly informing us.

Whether on the side of good or evil, we will always be fighting a war. *If we win, what do we win? What would it look like without the war?* The battle keeps us immersed in illusion. The illusion that someone will win and someone will lose. But there is no battle. It is Love that brings justice, not the fight.

The war continues as long as we defend and attack. Love does not attack or intimidate or overpower. Authentic strength does not challenge or move against, it preserves and sustains what is of value. Love purifies, cleanses, restructures, and harmonizes, stimulating revelation and emergence.

Grace occurs with the inclusion of and commitment to Love at its source. When we are drawn away from this, we "fall from Grace." We can live in the world of Love even as evil continues to play out around us. Our job is to withdraw our participation and lead others to do the same. Contact with Love will dissolve our confusion about what is true and real. It will purify our will so that we can be honorable, as is our nature.

We have learned that to make our way in this world we must do for ourselves and at the same time, we are asked to sacrifice the self, leading us to believe that it is correct to partake in things that are harmful. By receiving the judgement of "good" and "bad," we are brought to a place where we do this willingly. This is seen as service but does not resemble true service. Some manner of self-sacrifice appears to ensure our place. But a life lived for self-fulfillment, alternating with self-sacrifice, does not fulfill our longing. So far, the needs of society do not match the needs of the individual even though the society is made of individuals. We can be of service or we can play to an audience. We can't do both.

Evaluation of one's goodness relies on an arbitrary set of values that varies from one individual, one group, and one society to another. Goodness is a house of straw, and the wolf is ever ready to blow it down. We are both the pigs and the wolves, building and tearing down each other's provisional shelters by turn. We pick through the personality trying to fix the flaws with the scattered seeds of transitory goodness (at best). One blue ribbon must submit to the next, for goodness is never branded to us permanently. It is earned over and over because our soul is assumed to be tainted. We wash out the blood again and again.

TEMPTATION
The Seduction of Earthly Desire

The structure based on delusion boils us down to survival strategies and feeds our basic urges to keep us engaged. The enticement to fulfill these urges reinforces our sense of weakness and the feeling of being imperfect, sinful and incomplete. We explain that our pursuits are "natural" because at our core, we are of an animalistic nature. But when we boil ourselves down to biology we are doomed to succumb to our lowest impulses. We try to fulfill them without thought to how this affects our body and soul, trading in the enduring for the unenduring. There's only one thing that can fulfill us and it's not something we're chasing.

Becoming civilized or domesticated perpetuates the delusion, as it detaches us from the natural state, the natural order, the natural society. We are not mere biology, nor are we machines. The mechanistic view dissects, dehumanizes, denatures. The temptation that leads us to run with our base impulses has us believing that our participation in the false world is being rewarded.

Temporary satisfaction is a substitute for losing track of Truth and the bliss of mutual reception. Seeking to fulfill our cravings diverts us from fulfilling

our true needs. What make us feel powerless is the belief that there is nothing else. The outside world encourages us to grab 'n go, get our fill. By reducing us to the level of beasts propelled by impulse, we live out our lives as a fraction of what we are. Personal and collective trauma leads us to believe that there's nothing we can count on.

We know that we are not fulfilling our longing for freedom, integrity and mastery, so we seek out fleeting pleasures to mask our unsettled feeling. The need to flee from the agony of our unmet yearning drives us to seek stimulants and sedatives in alternation because our personal energy, when divorced from its source, is diminished. We drink coffee or tea to speed up, we smoke marijuana or take sedatives to slow down, and the restorative promise of sleep becomes elusive. These entrapments and discharges degrade our sacred body.

At the root of our submission to temptation is the drive for false power because we have lost track of what true power is. We seek worth through the accumulation of riches and recognition, stirring envy where we could instead feel inspired and animated toward collaboration. We are stimulated to compete for resources of all kinds. Lust for fulfillment drives us to possess and consume and to take what is not ours—to conquer rather than to merge. We know we are not free because nothing satiates—not the food, not the fame, not the beauty, not the sex, not the money. We are craving something else. *What is it?*

Freedom arises out of integrity and integrity arises out of incorruptibility. Sin means "to miss the mark" because we are missing the mark of where Love resides.

In our integrity we don't play a bartering game with Love. The more we lose touch with the realm of pure Love, the more we give in to our urges rather than mastering our awareness. Love is a place and a state of being found within the body where we feel both safe and free. The seduction to abandon enduring self-mastery for momentary pleasure is the way in which we are led astray.

If we recognize that we are integral to the whole, our choices, actions, perceptions will equal Truth and Love; if not, we will be out of harmony with Love, DISintegrated and acting from fear and a sense of isolation. Integrity is our protection. Otherwise, we are vulnerable to parasitic and predatory behavior, in both the physical and the astral. We are in search of a sustenance that seemingly can't be found.

Self-harm of all kinds sustains an environment that interferes with our potential for true embodiment. Following our impulses without self-awareness is to agree to this. It is to become the predator and the prey. We are asked, again and again, to rise to battle or succumb to decadence. *But who is leading us to Truth?*

If we are slaves to our urges, we are NOT free. Anything we cannot turn away from can be used to influence us. To recognize the power to choose, we begin by saying "no." Then we will know that our "yes" is a choice. When we have command over our choice to say "yes" or "no" we are incorruptible. When we fight the outer forces, we experience more and more disempowerment. Power is seen as out there, not within, and we can't access the power within as long as we don't see that what we are lusting after "out there" is counterfeit love.

Coming into the awareness of our *integral* role fulfills the longing and inspires us to share the richness of life because we can see and feel that we are a part of one another—borderless, indispensable. Integrity is not something we maintain with our will against all odds. True, abiding integrity is discovered at the interior and fulfills us to no end. It cannot be undermined because it represents our relationship to the whole.

It is at our source of pride that we are most blinded and therefore most vulnerable to manipulation when referring to our families, our worldly successes, our material rewards, our sexual prowess, our looks, etc. We can't see the truth about something to which we have submitted our definition of self. It is consent for a world in which the mercy of Love is missing.

Pride is taking ownership of something as representing oneself. This disassociates us from our human family, expanding our feeling of alienation and increasing our attachment to the identity that provides a sense of worth each time it is reinforced and worthlessness when it is overlooked. The need to be recognized and acknowledged creates dependency on how we are seen.

Transitory indulgences are consolation prizes for the unfulfilled longing. This longing causes us to lose mastery over our urges. The discovery of true fulfillment allows us to regain this mastery. In various esoteric practices, discipline is applied over impulses so that we may come to the discovery of Divine union. However, *it is possible for ordinary humans to come into union first*, with the byproduct being the mastery of primal urges.

What makes us susceptible to allurement, and ultimately control and manipulation, is the loss of interrelatedness. It appears as if Love does not exist. It's a dog-eat-dog world and there's not enough for everyone. False motivations arise out of the survival story. But it is only a survival story if we are alone. *Are we alone?*

How can we enter the experience of another if we are agitated by our urges and compulsions? Through engaging with the reciprocity of telepathic union, an act of discovery backed by our will, we can come to experience the truth of ONEness which leads to deeper fulfillment, allowing us to abandon the fruitless search for satisfaction where it can't be found.

To turn away from the destructive force of impulse is to know that we can engage with something greater in a *practical* way. The looping pursuits of short-lived pleasure bring us into karmic situations where our distance from Love is reflected back to us. This provides opportunities for course correction. If we don't have the freedom to choose, then we are not responsible for the way things turn out. We are at the mercy of forces outside of ourselves and, therefore, can blame our wretched state on things that are seemingly out of our control.

To avoid material seduction is not to attain perfection, but to *decontaminate one's motivations* in order to come out from under the influences

that obscure reality so that we can recognize that something we can sense and feel is listening and wants to be heard. It is to recall that there are ways of knowing that we can <u>trust</u> to guide us. When we set aside the self-compromise inherent in submitting to temptation, we open the door to assistance.

Chasing immediate gratification clouds our vision. Without clarity, we are subject to invasion. All those who are not self-possessed are other-possessed. When we are separated from our home, we are propelled by fear, which seeks the promise of safety and satisfaction by accepting the lollipop.[1] When we allow ourselves to be corrupted in this way, we participate in the lie of the false reality. If we can't walk away from the lollipop, we become the oppressor and the oppressed. But in TRUTH, we are in an ongoing conversation with consciousness. We are free.

When we are integrated within, congruent in our inner and outer functionality, we become sensitized to the needs and expressions of others *and ourselves.* We support each other's greatness with our own. This leads to a desire to serve, from which emerges the qualities we wish to cultivate in our children—responsibility, trust, compassion, integrity, authenticity, etc. Instead of teaching them how to *cultivate* these, we can lead them to Love so that they <u>become</u> them. Rather than teaching them how to be, we need only lead them home.

---

[1] *(The Lollipop)* "If you do this, I'll give you this."

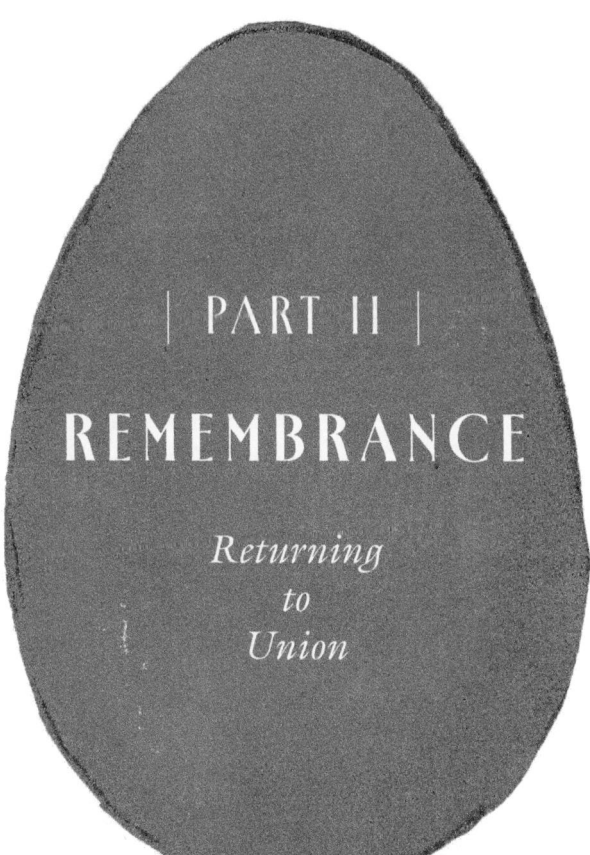

| PART II |

REMEMBRANCE

*Returning
to
Union*

CONFUSION OF REALMS
The Astral and The Ethereal

The Spirit of the human soul is delivered to earth inside its own ecosystem. This system is guided and enlivened by a power which intelligently adapts, moment to moment, to enhance and sustain life. All living beings are systems. All natural systems are living beings. These systems require a unifying communication network. The Ethereal realm is this network. It weaves together all things by way of fine filaments with contact points made of light, each representing an aspect of consciousness infinitely connected to other aspects.

The Ether encompasses our home. It is the dominion of the formless poised to be called into form through interactive awareness. It is the soil of reciprocity, the Internet within. It was created before time and cannot be broken. When we dream here, we re-vision the world. It is time to reorient ourselves toward this space.

The Ether lights up lines of communication between points of consciousness through directed awareness. It is a meeting place for all living beings to relate in the native language of the sensorial-imaginal. It is held together and called into formation by Love. Sensorial "sight" precedes thought. The translations of the intellect are designed to be of service to this primary faculty. Working in the Hypnogogic State paves the way for us to dive under the tyranny of the mind and find a clear space so that we can stimulate our sensing/feeling awareness as the illumined contact point we represent.

The fundamental reality responds to dedicated interaction amidst the interior network. The true matrix, or Mother, is this network that connects all of life—The Mother Web. She is within us and we are within her. We return here to discover Truth. When we find her and learn to stay with her, the karmic cycle ends, as its purpose was to move us back to Love. We can re-enter the womb, the inner chamber, while at the same time venturing outward. We need to do both to imprint Love upon the physical.[1]

The "Mother Web" places us amidst our immortal comrades. We are each embodied in the eternal womb, permeated by the ethereal fabric. We cannot become an integrated, highly functioning collective in service to mankind and the world until we embrace and reclaim the knowledge of the web of creation. We can cultivate this relationship to become a conduit for all that she represents

> Before I am born, I am within her and she is within me. After I am born I must remain within her still. As she is there for me, I come to know myself as her. There is bliss in the union. To receive the full care and nourishment of The Mother is to find the inner nourishment. At the moment when I am both The Mother and The Child, giving and receiving at once, I merge with Love.

---

[1] *refer to the practice* "Meeting Love" *in* **Part III: The Method**

and lead others here. The only cure for despair is to continuously return to this home. Through directed awareness, we invigorate our relationship with Love and are guided effortlessly. In elucidated contact, we engage only with what is real.

The *Ethereal Body* is the body within the body, a meeting place between the seen and unseen. It is the celestial interior. By occupying this space, we find power and inspiration. We find that we are protected and connected. This is where we strengthen our collective governance. We bring immortality to life through conscious engagement here, which directs Power into the mortal physical. To merge with the Ethereal is to extend in awareness beyond time and space.[2]

There are two ways to navigate to this home: We can shed the false persona to reveal the etheric body, which is Love. **Or** we can consciously engage with the ethereal and allow the false persona to fall away. The second is the fastest route to Love and Truth. When we find the love space *first*, all that we do emerges from Love and Integrity.[3]

The astral realm, by contrast, is a reflection of the hijacked human psyche. In the astral, we encounter thought projections acquired via the volatile conceptual reality. *What can we dream of when we are conceptually separated from Love?* Lovelessness, demons, witches, clowns, a world that lays us to waste. We are not engaging with Love when we expel the "spirit" into

---

[2] *refer to the practice* "Donning the Ethereal Body" *in* **Part III: The Method**

[3] *refer to the practice* "Meeting The Mother" *in* **Part III: The Method**

the astral. The escapades that occur here do not align with Truth.

The astral reflects and projects from the "overself," which experiences glorification and doom in alternation. It is the home of demons and angels, reflecting back an array of experiences according to the montage of beliefs, collective and personal, that move and shape the fictional "I". It is false sustenance for the solitary being who fends for himself.

All that we unconsciously and recklessly submit to keeps us bound to the astral and infused by corrupted forces. We engage with it through untethered awareness. In the astral we are offered the apparitions of a nightmare, vacillating with grandiose visions of self. We are haunted and vulnerable to psychic and energetic attack because The Temple is vacated. When we are fully embodied, in contact with Love, we are invulnerable to such harm.

We feed into the collective garbage can of the astral through unfettered rumination where it continues to haunt and taunt us, causing pattern disruptions within and around those whose identification points resonate toward and around it. This serves to further solidify the false creation of self, leading to DISease and DISharmony within ourselves and those around us. Contact with beauty, order, and harmony renovates these disturbances. When we are in direct contact with Love, we become a lens through which it sees and transmutes distortions of reality.

- Physical - seen
- Astral - unseen, illusory
- Ethereal - unseen, causal/communal, pure Love

The veil of self-image interacts in a world of projection and reflection because it is *not real*. Therefore, like narcissus peering into the pool, there is nothing to see or experience outside of the image adored. It subsists on ideas *about*. The authentic being has no need to see itself as anything. As the resolved separation, it has full access to the glory of the kingdom within. Pure perception disengages us from projection and reflection.

The astral is found *up and out*. We know we are there if we feel the need to invoke protection. Only fear asks for protection. When we are separated from Love and Truth, we are susceptible to the influence of thought patterns that form the basis of illusory experience.

> Two ways to interact with the world:
> - Projective/reflective (False reality)
> - Love, pure perception (True reality)

The more often we come into contact with Love, the more we align with the authentic essence and the less vulnerable we are to exploitive energies. Our powerlessness is an invitation for contamination. When we merge with Love, renovation begins and we become the vessel by which this is extended.

The astral is a product of the corrupted imagination. It is the unseen realm of the man-made consensus reality. Those who are powered from within are immune to the psychic harm of the astral, which is the dumping ground for the deluded and misdirected imagination throughout time. To extract ourselves, we must decline to engage in practices that do not come from deep within. When we exit the astral, karmic debt collapses and dissolves.

THE ONE AND THE MANY
Why and How Telepathy Occurs

Despite appearances, we are never acting in isolation. Like a leaf on a tree or an organ in the body, we each have a function to fulfill. A tree appears to be a singular entity but is made of many things and is also itself, a whole and a part of something larger. An organ in the body is the same. A heart is made of many things with varying roles that support its function while the heart also supports the function of something greater than itself. Every "one" has a function to perform within the whole. Every whole is made of individuals, every individual is a constituent of the whole. The community cannot be more important than the individuals in their function within it. Those functions ARE the community, therefore no individual shall sacrifice the self for the whole, as that makes the whole dysfunctional.

When we transcend the "I," we gain access to the greater organism as both The One and The Many. Recognizing that our place within this is *within us*, we can collaborate and direct The Power from which all aspects of expression originate. There is nothing to connect to because we are already a part of. There is simply something to notice. This is what makes telepathy possible.

As The One within The Many and The Many within The One, we are within that which is within us. We are the light and the dark, the incubation and the expression. We are the body within the body of the body within us. We are the vision within the vision. The tiny picture is the bigger picture and the bigger picture is contained within itself and vice versa. The illusion of separateness veils the interrelatedness that lies beneath. When we touch that with our sensing/feeling/knowing, we experience bliss.

Satan is a symbolic representation of the force that overtakes us when we are not aware of our undivided existence. There is nothing missing and nothing to compensate for. We are complete. Trustworthy forces are here to support our well-being. We find them when we discard the habitual for what is *natural*. The landscape of Love belongs to all. We can plant ourselves there and grow in Truth.

The One and The Many is a shared engagement of infinite points of consciousness working to receive and transmit information in service to the whole. Life is an expression of being but also an arrangement of united expressions. As The One and The Many, we are the interconnected soul.

The ultimate "ONE" is The Creator, of which we are all a part, an aspect by which unique perspective and planning emerge within the whole. This is the form that creator and creation take. When we see ourselves as singular, we are deceived. Manifestation is borne out of engagement with The One and The Many, operating in correspondence. Nothing real and true can be achieved without the ALL.

Most of us are not collaborating with life in full consciousness. We engage in the outer conversation without the inner conversation. When we let go of the solitary drive of limited resource, we engage with the greater power. Through the imaginal realm, we invite the power of The One and The Many to work with and through us.

As human beings moving from delusion toward Truth, what is available is reality design. The Vision is an aspect of creation that seeks to be fulfilled. What we find within is not private. The mission is shared. We are each an aspect of the one vision that contains the many "eyes" or vistas of infinite aspects of consciousness.

There is no "other," only facets and waves of expression. Therefore, to know and experience one another, other beings and the formless on the brink of form, we awaken to the truth that we are within one another and can direct our attention toward whichever part of the whole we wish to engage with. If we know that we are within all and contain all, we no longer prostrate ourselves to something greater or higher. We know that we can excavate what is needed from the field of Love because we are Love. What we seek is accessible. The "observer" is the true essence, connected to The One and The Many. The cosmic gypsie.

When we live in the physical world, we live on the plane of effects *from things that have come before*. Without contact within, we are merely reacting to what has been set forth, a world we did not create. Without our conscious interaction, the world of effects gets messy. Working on the causal level of the ethereal unseen, we can re-establish order, beauty and form in partnership with everlasting Love. There is work that must be done to shift the game. It is okay for us to intervene.

Sensing/feeling is a state of receiving by which interactive language can occur with The Many. We tether ourselves to this place through the inner sight of the sensorial, where we find that our energy is limitless. By way of this, we bring the purity of the inner world into the outer to cleanse all that it touches. Outer "pollution" has no power to contaminate this.

The overself is made of the past and future, the regrets, the pain, the separate, lonely journey, punctuated by false camaraderie. When we are aware of The Union we stop relying on this restricted power. We are the supported and the supporter, escorted through life by unerring wisdom. When we give up the lonely journey, the individual expands beyond self to a clear expression of his/her incomparable aspect of awareness that envisions and expresses in fully counseled form. No bargaining needed. Access was never denied.

Nature is a model for what is true. It provides a map that brings us to the treasure. Nothing is set apart. There is only <u>Inter</u>dependence. To enter and express in the masculine world out there we must pass through the Feminine (darkness, receptivity). The Masculine penetrates to deposit the seed, which is incubated in the womb space and nurtured into outward expression.

Darkness does not equate to Evil. Darkness is Love, care, safety, support, and the Truth found within

Nature's Womb. Light does not equal Love. Light is illumination of all that stands in the way of unification. Love encompasses dark and light. Darkness nurtures. It reveals what is Love and what is not Love.

It takes strength to come into the light. The light can be fierce and overwhelming. The darkness is soothing. It is a place to gather strength. We can't recognize wholeness if we believe only in the light. We can't come into a state of harmony if we seek only light. We must rest in the darkness to prepare for the light.

If we are operating from the unified whole, we find that everything is within us, including each other. When we look into the eyes of any being, we know that we are borderless. Looking into the eyes of another stimulates telepathic resonance. Eye contact helps us recognize our interconnectedness and stimulates the natural feeling/sensing abilities that transcend the physical.

We are immortal when we come into accordance with other points of consciousness. The agreement is to serve one another with sincerity, purity and humility. A "mortal" is one without access to internal power, a source that cannot be depleted. We are abbreviated via submission to the delusion.

When we step out of the overself as The One of The Many and The Many of The One, we can confidently establish a relationship to the inner collective. Through our integration with wholeness, we become the living prayer. As the living prayer, we draw peace, harmony, order, beauty into existence as the intersection point. Prayer arises from our connection to all beings who honor a desire borne of Love in service to the totality. We create and receive directives through our engagement. The sensation of inner touch draws Truth into the outer world.

The Knowing is accessible because of our "we-ness". The "We" is the wisdom that exists in all things and is accessible by way of internal collaboration. There is no me-ness. Me-ness is conditioning. We-ness is Truth. To get to we-ness is to clear the debris. The conscious rendezvous with other points of consciousness brings us to union. In the realization that we are The One and The Many, we align with our destiny and the manifestation of Love becomes effortless. *What do we long to see in the world?* We must move to take up this endowment.

In wholeness we are greater than the solo self. When a tree is sickly, it does not say, *"Well, I will just be the best tree I can be and I will heal."* No! It reaches its roots out farther for nourishment; it sends them deeper to draw on the support of the forest. We have denied ourselves this nourishment.

SACRED ARCHITECTURE
The Living Temple

There's a conversation that takes place in a sacred space we call the body, which is both physical and ethereal, and is the arena from which we inform and are informed. Though the body appears to be a personal vessel, it is a bridge between worlds. It houses our engagement with creation and leads us to the portal by which we come into active alliance with other conscious agents, each containing the wisdom of an incomparable source.

The body transports us to the inner cosmos. It is the link to the inner reality, which is connected to the cosmos and all of life. This is why it is sacred. This is why it is The Temple. When we enter the body, we transcend its limits.

The embodiment of the human soul is Love's lifeline to harmonization of the miscreations of fear. We become "lucid" when we see that thoughts are interactive and we can direct them to affect reality as both the receiver and the transmitter. Our ultra senses are roused through occupation of the body.

The Temple is subject to desecration when we fail to recognize what it is. When we power ourselves from the outside, our energy is in short supply. It is exhausting to manage an image of self and to be cut

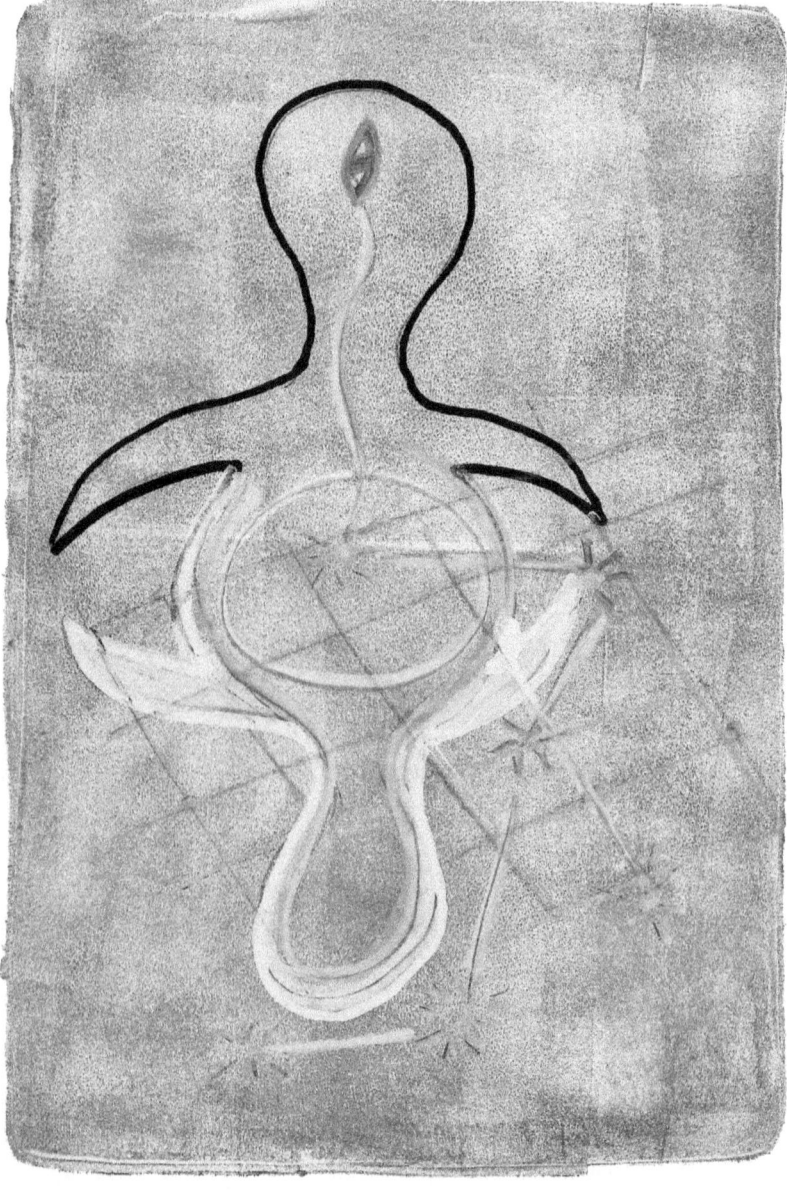

off from the true supply. The source of all power is limitless and needs no protection. Exploring the inner landscape is as much a communal affair as what we find in the outer. It is not a personal journey. It is not restricted to your individual person.

Psalm 91 *rewritten*

Whoever dwells in the shelter of Love from within the Temple rests in the womb of The Mother.

We will say of Love, "She is my refuge and my fortress in whom I trust."

Love will save us from the fowler's snare and the deadly pestilence. Love covers us with her feathers, and under her wings we find refuge; her faithfulness is our shield and rampart.

We will not fear the terror of night, nor the arrow that flies by day, nor the pestilence that stalks in the darkness, nor the plague that destroys at midday.

If we say, "Love is our refuge," and we make The Temple within our dwelling, no harm will overtake us, no disaster will come near our tent.

For she will command her cohorts to guard us in all our ways; they will lift us up in their hands so that we will not strike our foot against a stone.

We will partner with the lion and the cobra; we will come to know the great lion and the serpent.

The Power that flows from within the body reaches into many dimensions at once like an explosion of fireworks traveling through space and time. The dimensions we travel are not other places, they are what we are made of. They allow us to surf across other forms of life and enter and exit them as they also enter and exit us. If we recognize the practical value of this, we gain access to a giant toolbox.

In the False reality, the body is an object, which is how we come to see one another and ourselves. We are taught to mistrust our bodies and to hand them over to a higher authority. Almost everything that is happening in the world has the effect of taking us out of the body. If we live outside the body, within the projected mind, there will be little to sustain us. To "heal" is to heal the distortions that the clown show has placed upon the body through the disruption of

our awakened attention. The body falters in response to the hidden contract that unguided awareness enters into unknowingly—the unchosen, default reality.

Within the consciousness of the body is everything we want to engage with. It is the entrance to the integrated reality, joining us to the interior of the exterior. What we worship by our conscious presence within it is life itself. The vessel is intelligent, aware, interactive and equipped to inform us of how to care for it. The False World obscures this.

All that exists of us is our awareness. When there is no "me" to protect, the mental gymnastics are no longer of interest. Boundaries give way because they were never there. To tap into the unconstrained power of Love, we let go of the limited personal power and open to the greater field.

Nothing deep and soulful passes through one to the other unless we meet from within. The perception of a finite body, a finite world, is a fiction. When we withdraw from the fiction and return to the kingdom, we find that we have <u>not</u> been harmed and we are not broken. The Temple is intact, whole, functional, connected. All is WELL. Wellness is drinking from the well of origin.

We need to stay and occupy the space that is our home. This is how we revoke all permissions that were never granted. The inner world is the origin of matter. Our earthly vessel is the instrument that harmonizes as the living essence at work in the physical/material.

It takes practice to surrender to embodiment, since this is not what we are used to. The mind is typically hypervigilant, anticipating and predicting what it needs to protect itself from. When we are embodied, we are empty and available to what is, as it is. Our responses come from a larger arena that is orchestrated by internal wisdom. We exist beyond the boundaries of the body *by way of the body* as the motherland of creation.

The body is a community of which we are a part. It is both physical and ethereal and provides a pathway for correspondence. To step into it with our inner sight is to enter the immortal passageway. We can look outward with the physical eyes and we can look inward with the sensorial "eye." Both are real. We can access the nest of the magical apothecary from the celestial temple of the inner ethereal body. It requires the trust of a child's heart.

What matters to the being within the Temple is Truth and Love. There is nothing that anyone can give "you" that will fulfill you. Pride serves the figment. Lust serves the figment. Greed serves the figment. All are attempts to extract something out of life that doesn't satisfy or serve. In pursuit of these things, the figment is unreliable. We cannot *make* ourselves become something we're not, we can only extinguish what is not real. To live from within The Temple is to reclaim integrity.

The function of Love is to bring beauty, harmony and order. When you retract from what is not Love, you become a medium for Love, inviting others to enter The Temple where Love can be found.

We experience joy in the body when we devote ourselves to its care. We worship life through the body. The life and love that are in us are all around us.

From within The Temple, we are guided by the distinctive viewpoint of what we are and what is encoded there. We can seek guidance and perspective from other facets that are accessible from within or without. We take command of our will to occupy The Temple and when we occupy The Temple, we can take command of our will to excavate Love from the depths of the interior. This is the resurrection.

Offer yourself for full erasure by returning to The Temple. It doesn't have to be painful because it was never real. We call this ego death, but nothing dies. We simply extract ourselves. Ego death is a choice facilitated by a willing heart, a choice that is easily made when we see that we give up nothing. To say that there is ego involved means that there is attachment to an image that interferes with the ability to see our destiny. Love is our only nourishment. The ego must collapse for us to experience how powerful we are.

The embodiment of separateness is the false self. The embodiment of union is Love. As soon as we agree to the extinction of the distorted self, the separation ends. When this agreement occurs, awareness shifts from looking into the looking glass at the self to looking outward, directly at reality, which is how we exit the delusion (dilution). To become lucid in the collective reality we perceive it directly.[1]

---

[1] *refer to the practice* "Resolving the Separation" *in* **Part III: The Method**

FAITH AND TRUST
New Lines of Sight

We fear because we see a world that doesn't make sense. We fear ourselves and others, seeing that we are capable of great harm through our detachment from Love. Through Faith we can find Love even if we are living in Fear. When we recognize the underlying reality, Divine powers become accessible.

In the illusory world, our lives are chaotic and the more trauma and drama we encounter, the less we listen and the worse things get because we are out of contact with the fundamental order. The oscillations of the intellect drown out the sacred silence because we have applied our faith to believing in *ourselves*. Everything that stands in our way is false perception. Our eyes look outward but what is real is found with the inner, sensorial eye and must inform the outer for Truth to be our chaperone. Faith was abandoned because Love is hidden behind an elaborate set.

Faith and Trust reveal the true reality. With no map to the hidden, we are sent into the material without understanding how to utilize the forces that shape it. Access to the interior infrastructure is obscured. If we don't seek, it will not be found. If we don't "know", it cannot be accessed. If we don't ask, it cannot be

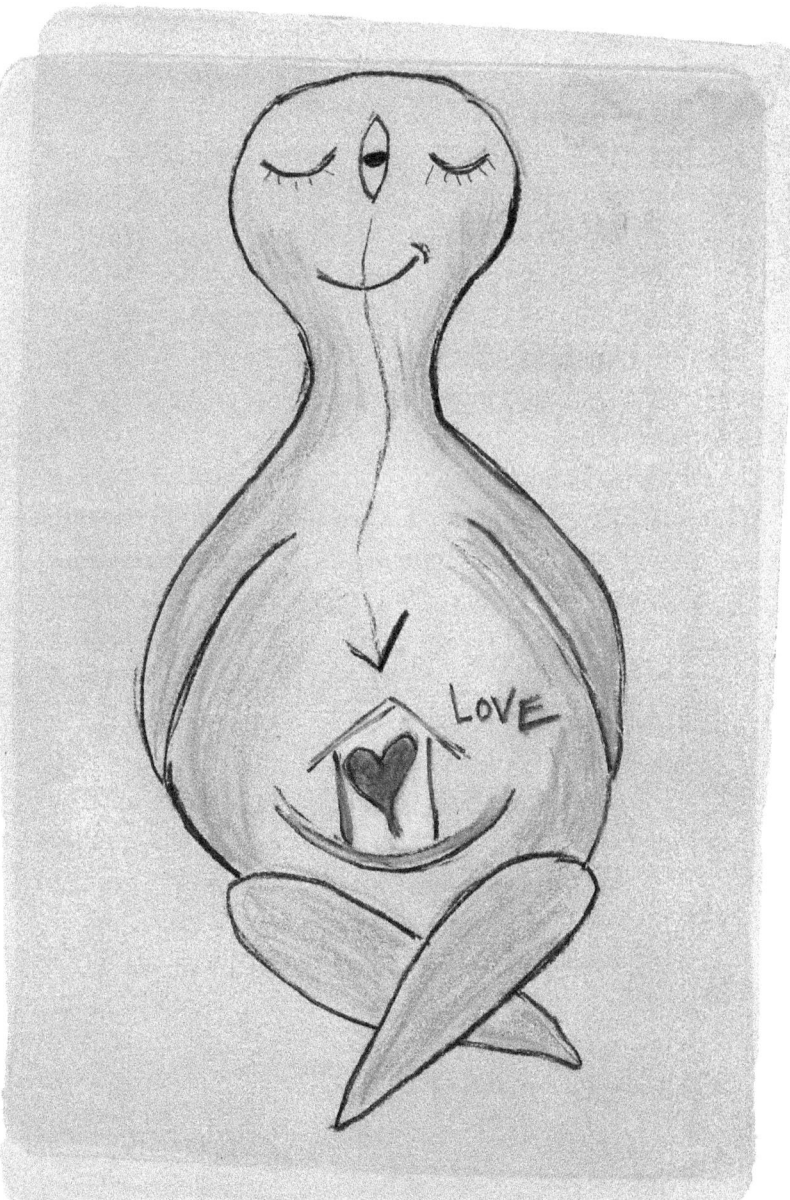

received. Trust/Faith will reveal it as something we can see, feel, know.

The Faith that is needed is faith in our nature, our innocence, our connection to the power of creation. Our Faith is not for God, but for mankind. By way of Faith, we seek, allowing us to find. By way of Faith, what is hidden is revealed.

Many will say they have Faith because they "believe in," but the only way to have <u>Functional Faith</u> is to trust. <u>Functional</u> means trusting deeply enough to be led to the access point where all that we yearn for exists in infinite potentiality.

As we surrender to Faith—that we are loved, taken care of, guided and connected to something larger—we shed our dependency on false pleasure and are able to find Love. Our addictions are not about a lack of self-control or even trauma; they are about separation from Love. Discipline paves the way for us to recognize our wholeness. *The discipline to do what?* **To enter The Temple and find Love.**

Faith requires courage. It is going forward as if we are protected, as if there is a solution, as if a creator exists. Faith arises from our sincerity, which purifies our intent. This allows us to step onto the path, and as we do, the path rises to meet us. With Faith we find our way. The Love is already ours. Healing is recognizing our connectedness through Trust. Purification is shedding what is not true.

BLURRED ALTARS
The Quest for Enlightenment

Many spiritual pursuits and studies are causing us confusion. The purpose of spiritual development is to gain mastery over our awareness so as to have access to the power of Love. We must question ideas about spirituality if happiness, peace, understanding and naturalness are largely unattainable. The purpose of spiritual "practice" is to bring us home.

Enlightenment is to lighten one's load. It is to relinquish what is not true. The load is our level of participation in the deception. Love and compassion are not accessible to a select few who achieve enlightenment. If they can be reached by one, they can be reached by all because to be reachable, they must be within the very nature of each and every one of us.

We don't have to become a spiritual devotee to find eternal Love. The long road is to purify the mind and body so that we can catch glimpses of Love. The short road is to go directly to where it is found and purification of the mind and body will follow because we are no longer impoverished.

But many are being led *up and out*, away from the inner sanctum where the convergence occurs and our original language is encountered. We are told we must go *up* to the heavens, *up* to enlightenment, *up* in vibration. The push upward is misleading. The real movement is toward integration. A rendezvous with the imperishable home. This integration is magnetic, as it is a reminder to others of something they have known. We can see and feel "home" in one another.

To integrate, we must go down. The tunnel, the void, the source of Knowing is a backward launch down and in. From here we are bright and alive, carried and nurtured by an inner fountain. In here we unite and are blissfully received. Come in and wait. It takes a second or less. Faster than McDonald's.

Even amidst spiritual pursuit, the underlying conversation can be overlooked because we are trained in the pursuit of specialness so that we continue to waffle back and forth between self-aggrandizement (I am chosen, special, set apart, vibing high) and depression (I am nothing, nowhere, nohow). Back and forth we go, puzzled as to why we feel great one moment and worthless the next.

Our true blossoming is about our degree of realness in connection with Love. The more ties we discard to the false self and the false reality, the more embodied we become, the more present, the more magnetic because in our state of origin, we recognize ourselves as an essential ingredient of the greater form. Our magnetism is related to our level of authenticity. The concept of a "high vibration" is a metaphor with nothing tangible to aim for. If we know that our authenticity is directly tied to our ability to touch down into the place and state of being that is Love, then we know that we can choose this and ultimately never leave. When we refer to the raising of our vibration we are not offered a practical reference point for how that is achieved or why it occurs.

The Dark Night of the Soul ensues when we stumble upon Home for a quick minute but we don't know how we got there or how to return. We reach again for the false prize, *"I am magnetic." "I am beautiful." "I am enlightened." "My vibration is high."* We are sucked back into the possibility of goodness or even greatness and from there we fall into the dark and are lost. We are back in the game that can't be won. The pursuit of false prizes. Close your eyes and sink down in, lower and lower.

Synchronicity is often thought to be a sign that we have done something right. But what synchronicity reveals is that we are in conversation with consciousness. If an eagle lands on our porch, if we find feathers on the ground, if we see triple or repeating numbers, these are conveyances within an ongoing dialogue. When we enter into the conversation, we can respond!

Telepathic communion allows us to incorporate the qualities of deities or animal spirits or to call councils and guardianships into form to assist us. These are examples of collaborations that can occur, which include telepathic communion with humans, animals, plants, and more. We "commission" the unseen by consciously intersecting with it drawing on the wisdom of The Many. The entire natural world is available for conversation.

> **Myth:** To earn love through admiration = worthiness
>
> **Truth:** We are each a one-of-a-kind facet within the mosaic of our interconnected destiny

Our longing and search for more arises because *a world of Love **does** exist*. We are the igniters and the inviters. Our reverence is expressed through "being with" and faith in wholeness, which brings us toward our integral ability to consciously create. There is nothing to which we must prostrate ourselves. Sentimentality serves no purpose.

Interfacing with the treasures of the inner world changes the outer world. At the base of all yearning is the desire to express life as we have been designed to. *How many spaces can we feed with the pulsing blood of Love?* There are infinite branches.

Spiritual pursuit leads to glimpses of something greater but not enough to lead us directly to Truth. There is a simple and available path back home. Spiritual practice is cultivating the confidence and curiosity needed to seek and find, to reach in to other facets of knowing and trust in the wisdom and collaborative urges that arise. We need to respond to these beckonings with dedication. Then we will see that we are rightly guided. Love connections converge through alliances that offer a glorious place for every One.

When we believe we are not from here or do not belong here, our disassociation increases our longing. Focusing on being from another planet, another time,

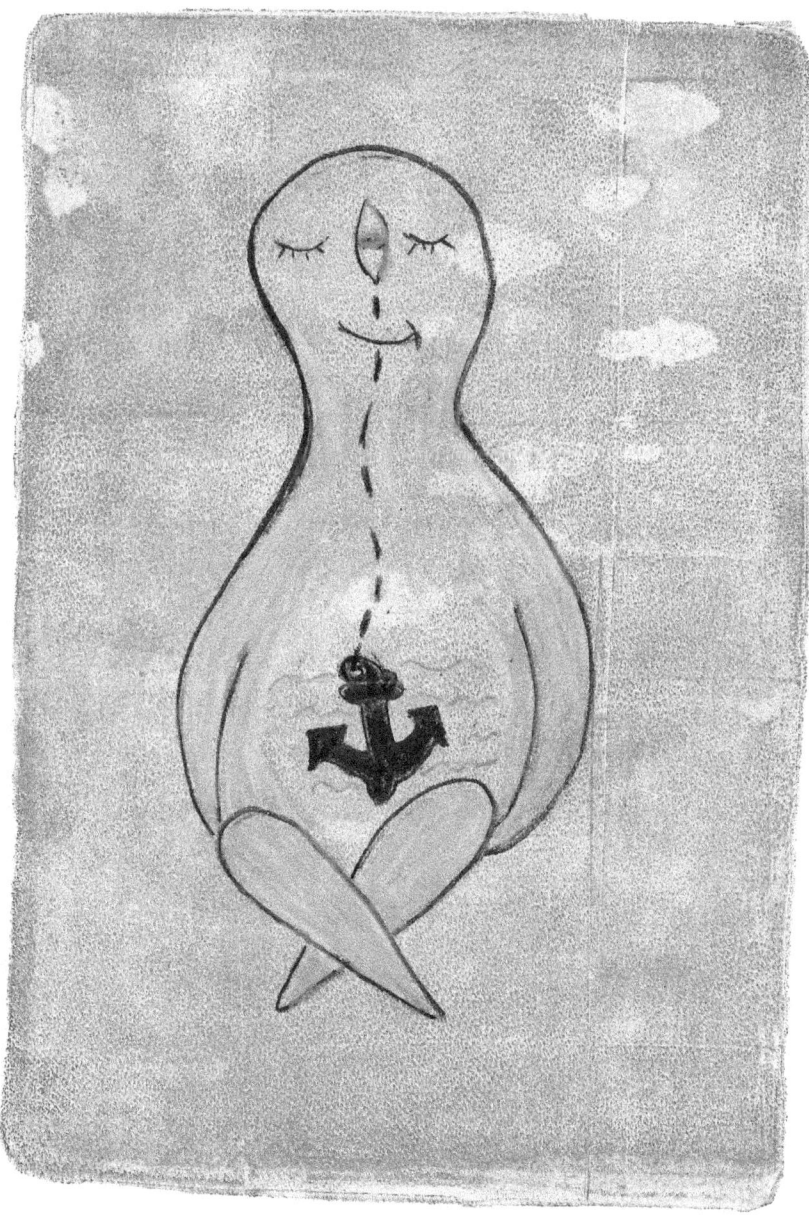

another place and not wanting to be here is a part of the delusion that separates us from the collaborative work that must be done to provide a more welcoming world for our children and our human brothers and sisters.

LOVE AND TRUTH
There's No Place Like Home

"Love is the only reality and it is not a mere sentiment. It is the ultimate truth that lies at the heart of creation."
— Rabindranath Tagore

The overuse and misuse of the word and concept of Love has drawn us away from understanding what it is and how it can be encountered and upheld. Love is the language we have always known. It is the deepest union. It is both a place and a state of being. *When we enter the place, we come into the state of being* so that all that we give and receive arises out of Love and Truth.

Love is conscious, interactive and wants the best for all. We seek Love

> Once upon a time, we lost track of Love and began to think and feel as if we were "not-love." Not-love took on a life of its own, making not-love palatable and keeping Love invisible. The beings of Love waited patiently for us to return, but we couldn't find them because we didn't know something had been lost. Our longing drove us to seek but we didn't know where to look. We sought and sought and the pain of our eviction remained. We participated in a lie because we didn't know that Truth existed. We could no longer make sense of the world.

so that we can direct reality. False riches must be left behind. We are either *in* or *out*. Cross the bridge and don't look back.

Love and Truth emancipate us, allowing us to step into our roles as guardians of humanity and life on earth. If this does not emerge naturally, then we have been misled. In the close-up view, it seems as if what is right before us is the agitator. When we pan back, we see that our awareness is constrained. But from the expanded view, we can find our way out, which is in.

> *Why do we need to access Love/Truth?*
> - To resolve our despair
> - To learn that we are supported and guided
> - To hear our calling and fulfill our destiny
> - To experience bliss, renewal, peace and safety
> - To collaborate with other aspects of consciousness
> - To take part in the telepathic communication network

When we align with Truth, the search for self-glorification ends. It is electrifying to come across our place in the synergistic tapestry by accessing the unique aspect and function of consciousness we are here to fulfill. We can help each other bring these expressions about. When we have met Love and united with that state, we have no choice but to represent Truth because the two are inseparable.

> From the state of Love, you are not beholden to me. I would ask you to come into your greatness and serve you toward that end. I would reflect your beauty back to you. I want to love you in your strength. I want to look upon your grandeur.

To thrive, we must integrate with one another. Integration allows us to synchronize with others by piecing together our skills, talents, aptitudes and wisdom. Through unification, we are protected. Love provides the structure. We can all be propelled by internal passion and a desire to meet the world in a state of unity.

Humans are wise, innocent, and loving. This is our true nature. Evil occurs in the absence of Love. Our greatness is in direct proportion to our level of integrity. Our level of integrity is determined by our awareness of what is false or true. Integrity is unification with Truth.

When we know how to enter the state of Love, we renounce the pull of temptation and place integrity above all else. In this state, we don't need schooling on how to treat one another. We don't need a moral code. Nor do we need to define morality relative to our beliefs. We simply move away from the renderings that deceive us.

As Love, our awareness is a beam of light that shines on what is not aligned with Truth to bring it back to order. We don't banish the darkness, we become the illumination. We can direct this force. We can draw forth assistance and inform reality with the images that weave through the imagination, *the communal space of creation*.

In the state of union, Love sets to work on everything and anything that enters our presence and awareness. Awareness or attention is like the head lamp that shines a beam on all that it touches, initiating renewal. The more Truth we let in, the more peace and harmony come into our lives. This correlates to our level of "identification." The less identified we are, the more we can "see" and therefore respond to *what is*, rather than fiction.

What is false makes us feel small and powerless. Most of the information we consume is false and does not have the intention to solve problems, uplift, enliven, or call us to right action. Declining the temptation of *simulated fulfillment* leads to protection. We are protected by the choice to trust. When we see that we are held in Love, fear vanishes and we are no longer vulnerable to depletion. Love is seemingly inaccessible when we are DEnatured, boiled down to biology and diminished by our lowest urges in our acceptance of the material as divorced from spirit.

Much of what we find "out there" is rooted in deception though it may contain threads of Truth. Without the netting of Truth, lies disintegrate. A lie can appear to be Truth when spliced together with it. Truth is the scaffolding upon which lies are held. Truth feels safe and lies frighten us. Lies set upon Truth make us uneasy.

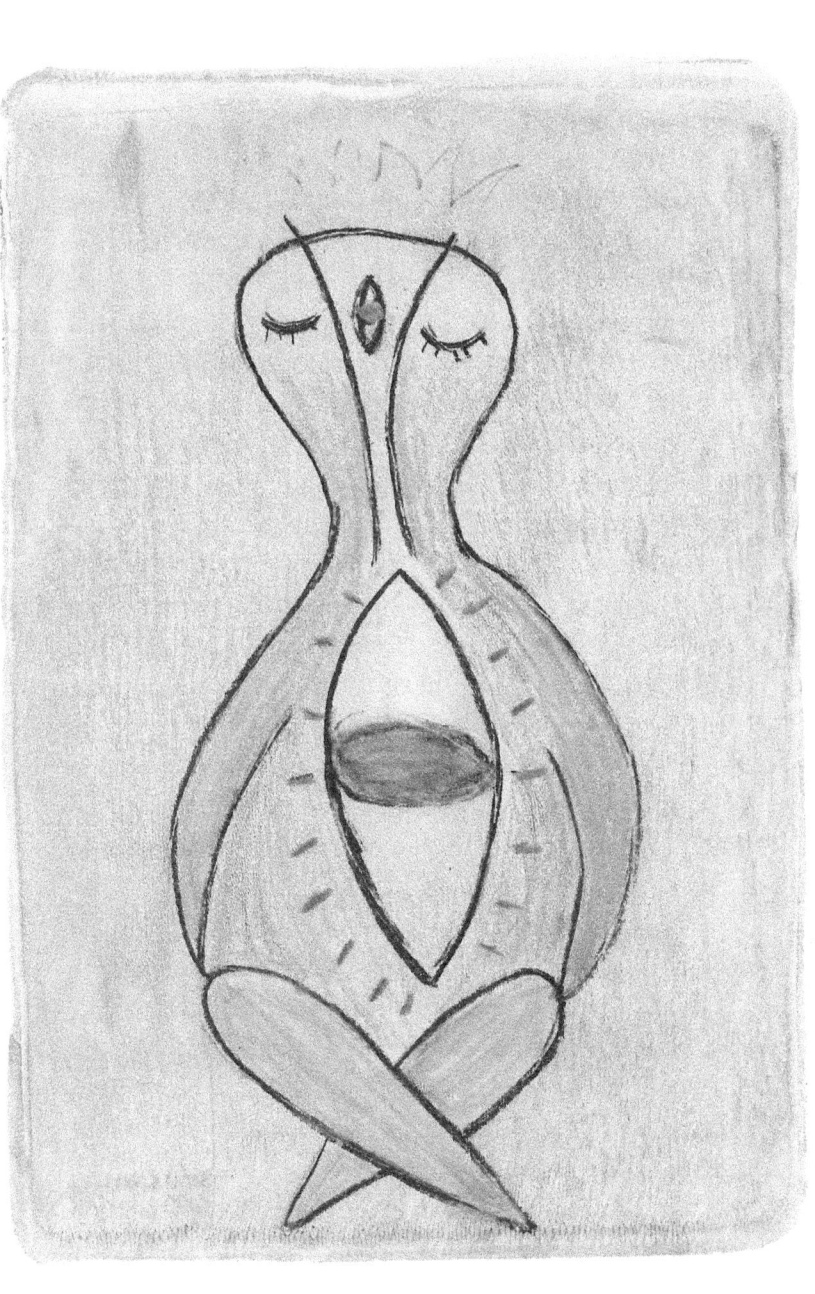

Truth not only supports us but informs us with knowledge that has practical value in shaping and responding to the world. In Truth, we are unified. Truth creates ease. It leads to purification and growth. Truth/Love is simple and does not confuse or disparage. It does not separate or ask us to prove our worth. When we find it, we know that it is with us wherever we go. Those who are willing to risk everything for Truth are operating outside of the system. We can transcend the perceptual distortions that hide the Truth.

Love leads us to the knowledge of our innocence and our place within the whole. What is real brings us toward Love. What is false moves us away from Love.

Truth can't be spoken because it is life becoming itself, a mystery awaiting our engagement and our <u>directives</u>. As we write the story, the story writes itself. The Truth feels like something we know. In Truth, we do not want to harm one another, we want to uplift one another and amalgamate characteristic expressions into the intrinsic whole. We haven't had the chance to choose this yet.

There is no need to devour anything as if it is our last pleasure, our last joy, our last meal. When LOVE is accessible as fulfillment, completeness is achieved. There is nothing to do but serve and create. Love's presence is obscured by things that are not Love, including what occurs in our thoughts. Thought divorced from Love upholds Evil. If we feel that we have been cast out, then our choices lead to self-compromise and self-destruction. We may live a "good" life but feel a sense of yearning and despair.

> What obscures Truth?
> - The artificial self
> - The interception of imagination

Love is where we anchor ourselves and are sustained by continuous rejuvenation. We are each a portal to a world filled with Love. In contact with Love, we become aware of the immense space we occupy. When we occupy this space, no one needs to tell us what is right.

Love is our dope. It offers fulfillment and shows us how to shape reality. When we contact Love, we are humbled by the vastness of our collective power and potential.

> Our unGodly choices created a mirage. And like maggots feed on dead bodies, parasitic beings fed on the rot of loveless choices. The world we have been given, that is supported by the provisions of the earth, was expropriated by the hijacking of free will via the imagination. Free will is not free if Love cannot be found. The more we degenerate, the more obscure Love becomes. All manner of methods have been deployed to lead us off the scent. Ridicule and ostracism keep us centered in the self, seeking nourishment through substitution. We know that we are more than this and yet we may not know where to look for Truth. Many cannot abide by the loveless nature of the false world and seek to escape.

Strong, inner-directed beings cannot be exploited, and, most importantly, will not exploit. True freedom is exiting the "getting" game to reach the place where all is a gift. We don't need to cultivate attributes like courage or compassion, they are already within us. Everything we need will flow from the ignited inner sun by way of contact with Love and Truth.

Consciousness is under our command when we solve the separation by coming into contact with Love. When we access the state of Love, we want to lead others there. The pure heart has access to the greatest power of all and never uses this to have *power over*. Taking command of one's awareness means sending it to the bottom of the ocean and partnering up with Love/Truth where human beings are invited to act upon physical reality via the reciprocal imagination.

We experience our essential desires when we are in contact with reality. First, we establish the relationship, then we allow it to guide and nourish us. Love oversees the cohesive functioning of the whole.

When we return to the coherent state of being from which we originated (and have never left), we pledge to honor Love with our receptivity and responsiveness across dimensions. We do not have to participate in false realities or artificiality. We are made of Love, therefore only Love can reach us. We return to the perfection of The Creator to follow the guidance of the heart and soul.

CLOSING
*The Road to Recovery:
Our Defining Moment*

We are the founders of the new reality. Either we define the moment or the moment defines us. Man's glory will not come by way of self-definition, but through an alliance with the infinite potential of the greater network of consciousness. When we surrender the one, small life, we become one with the power of Love, fluid and borderless. Collaboration with the unseen is essential for reality creation. The only way to create worlds is TOGETHER. Our shared destiny is fulfilled through union.

How do we build the world of our dreams? First, we notice the nightmare. Then we can learn how to withdraw our participation. Setting ourselves upon the inner road leads to the outer road. Building the new dream will dismantle the nightmare.

Evil is the wounded expression of human nature. To return to the bounty we give up nothing but weakness, defense, the confusion of lovelessness. We are not here to feel love, we are here to BE Love. Our calling continues to beckon whether we hear it or not. The Devil stands at the gate of heaven making promises. He uses our talent, our beauty and our charm to recruit others. We can each continue to lead the world astray or we can lead it back to Love.

It is not that we have lost our innocence, it is that we have *lost touch* with our innocence. When our passion and associated wisdom are submerged, we move toward the prescribed path instead of the felt path, causing us to overlook our essential part in the larger composition. It is necessary for our mutual health that we each find our function.

The integral human life is sensitive, kind, loving, supportive, inspiring, encouraging, curious, collaborative, strong, courageous, INNOCENT, and wise. When expressing our true nature, we are liberated. What is granted is alignment with our destiny, a mission that can be fulfilled by NONE *other* than you.

Whatever consciously and purely occupies the imaginal space directs the God force. This force wishes to serve in partnership with other forms of consciousness. Our collective is meant to be inclusive of the allies of the unseen, who want to assist in expediting The Vision. Through directed awareness, Love enhances and harmonizes all that our vision touches. Love requests that we surrender the game of pretending that we are anything other than Love.

If there is something out there that can give or take energy, exhaust us, make us feel powerless, then we are conceding that our power lies outside of ourselves and is dependent on others, circumstances or things gone right or wrong. NO. We are not weak, small or dependent. There is no MY power or your power. There is only one power that sustains and flows

CLOSING

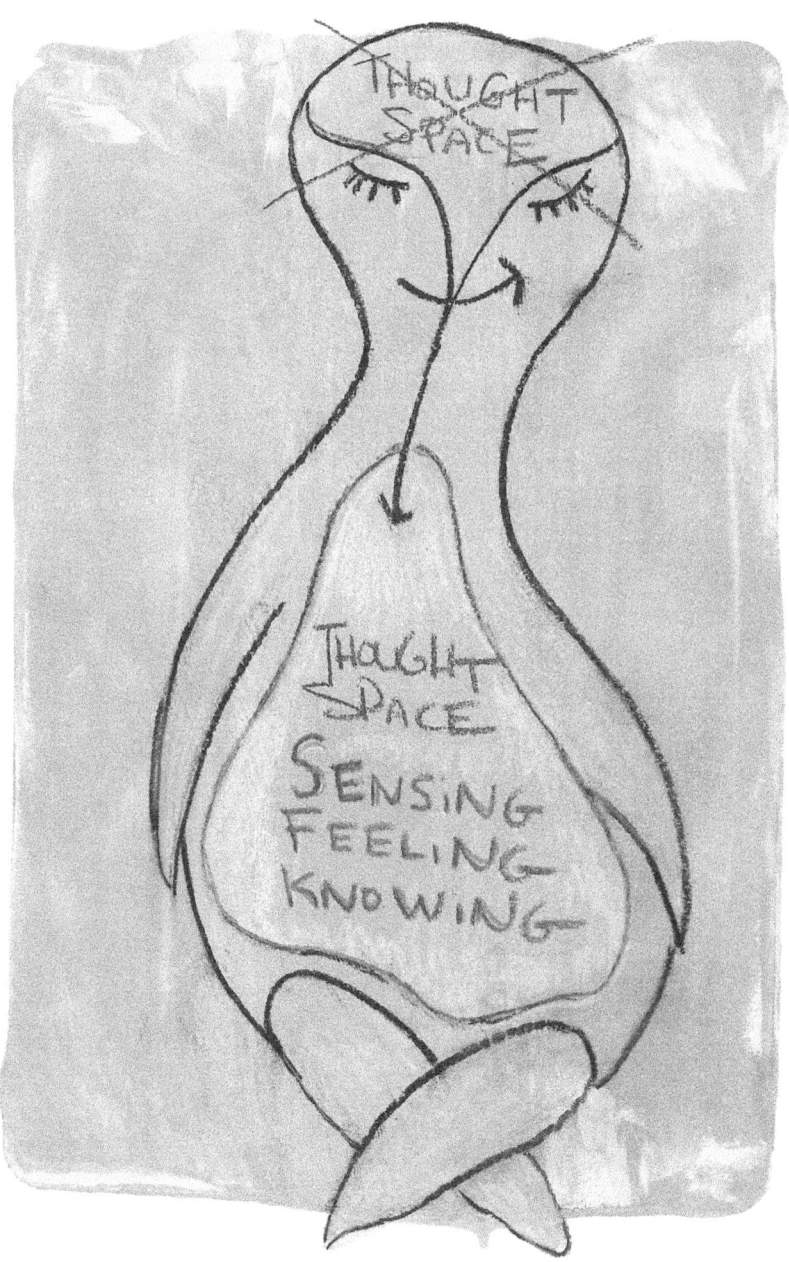

through. The source is endless and never waivers. It is steady and deep. It is the power to create in union with Love.

> **What do we need to do?**
> - Activate The Knowing
> - Communicate in our native language
> - Accelerate the birth of a just and merciful world
> - Let go of harm derived from participation in false ideas
> - Learn how to shape the world in union with other aspects of consciousness

Here is the defining moment. The time to step out of the game and know what we are connected to. Now is the time to see it, feel it and celebrate it. If we understand our world as conscious and recall that it is ever at the ready to engage, then we will understand how our interactions support the material world. Through conversations with other points of consciousness, we give birth to the new reality, fully supported by Love, Truth, and innate compassion.

PART III

THE METHOD

*Tools
for
Transformation*

The following are methods for exploring the inner terrain and engaging through telepathic communion. I present these exercises in the approximate order of my own discovery with the understanding that what I want to share can emerge through this process.

The following mini practices can prepare you for a sense of embodiment and inward focus and you can do them anytime, anywhere:

- Take a deep breath and hold it while you squeeze the perineum (anus, sex organs). Hold for as long as you feel comfortable. Release and breathe normally. *This allows you to feel into the deepest part of your body.*
- Sitting up straight with your eyes closed, bow your head for several minutes. *This practice relaxes the heart. For a deeper sense of reverence, you can hold your hands in prayer form.*

There are two kinds of awareness or attention:

- **Thought awareness**
- **Sensorial awareness**

In our typical state we hold thought in the foreground and relegate sensing/feeling to the background. To prepare our attention for the ethereal, we want to bring sensing/feeling to the foreground and relegate thought to the background.

All of these exercises are designed to move you away from the mind's eye and into the sensorial "eye" of the body. It can feel as if you are submerging yourself in the ocean, floating, and must find your way by feeling instead of with sight.

Hypnogogic Suspension. The best time to practice this is bedtime.

Lie flat on your back with your palms up. Do not cross your legs. Take a slow breath IN as if you are drawing it up from your belly. Push the OUTbreath downward into the body alongside your awareness. Allow it to pull you deep into the interior of the body. Do this three times slowly. Keep your focus immersed in the body after the last breath. Continue to breathe gently. Imagine that you are blindfolded and the body is a dark room. To experience what is in there, feeling and sensation are your tools. Imagine that your belly/abdomen/womb area is a resting place like a soft nest. Let the lower belly area receive you like a warm bath. If the mind engages elsewhere at any time, repeat the three slow breaths in the same way. You can also squeeze the perineum to bring your awareness deeper into the body.

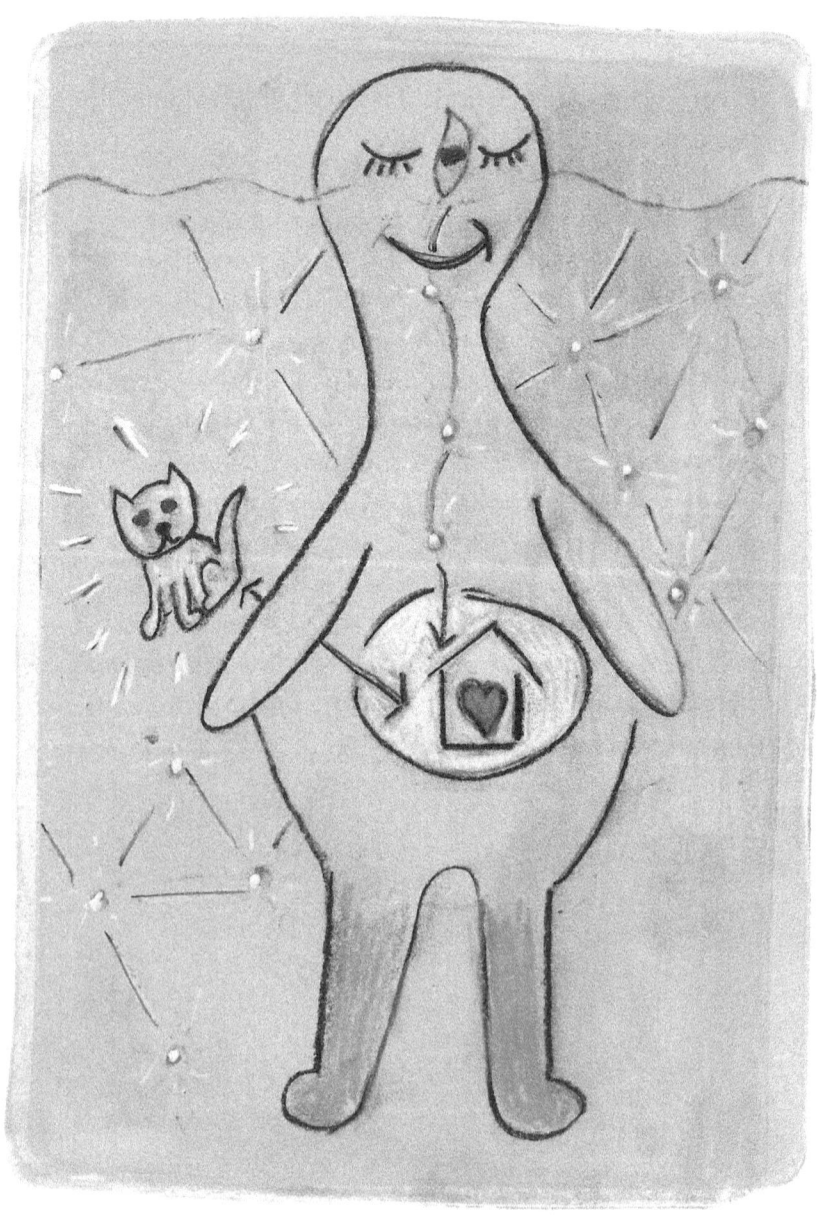

Inviting presence.

Choose an animal that you want to join with. Follow the previous instructions to enter the transitional state. When you have settled into the belly/womb area, use the OUTbreath to deepen the connection, pushing your awareness down and in toward the sacrum. Anchor yourself with this sensation. Imagine you are blindfolded, so that sensation becomes your "sight." Let your awareness travel slightly to the left, where a presence can appear from. Bring the animal to awareness with a name, feeling or characteristic. Relax into the body as if it is an empty bowl, open and receptive. Hold the dual awareness of the animal alongside the relaxation. Keep breathing slowly, softening with each breath. When relaxation begins to feel soothing or even euphoric, as if you are floating or being held, you will know that you are in conversation with the animal. You may also feel a buzzing or tightening between your eyes or on the forehead. The third eye buzzes when inner sight is aroused. Allow yourself to experience this for as long as you can.

When awareness joins with the body, nothing that occurs within it can harm you. No protection is needed because it is The Temple of Love. By entering the body, we exit the astral. At times, you may feel the weight of the heart wall, but please don't mistake this for a malefic force. It is the feeling of separation, which we will work to resolve in one of the exercises. There are ways to bypass the heart wall and enter into the womb space directly. One way is to come in from behind by bringing the awareness down the outside of the spine and entering the body through the sacral area.

Engaging in conversation.

Follow the instructions for the previous exercise. Once you feel the presence of the animal, you can initiate a silent conversation as if you're talking to a person. You can direct the communication with inquiries and requests. You can start with the question "What would you like to show me or tell to me?" TRUST *that you are in active conversation. Immerse yourself without trying to "get" anything. You can merge with the animal's body to feel what they want to show you. The more openly you receive the communication, in whatever form, the livelier and more expanded the conversation becomes. You can base other questions off of the responses. You can also ask "yes"/"no" questions. A yes will come faster than you can finish the question. A "no" often comes in the form of no response or a feeling of resistance. Responses can take the form of visual metaphors, as well as sensation. The process is like the slow reveal of an inkblot, starting off like a little spot and spreading into something that takes up more and more space. Answers may bring you on a journey that is similar to a dream. Everything conveyed is a real and active communication. (You can test this by asking the animal to show you they received this communication in some specific way. For this to work, you will need to explain why you are asking them to do this.)*

Meeting Love.

Lie on your back in complete relaxation as in all previous exercises. Keep your legs <u>uncrossed</u>. Move your attention to the deepest space of the inner womb—man or woman. Bypass the heart wall and any blockages of the mind by entering from behind, if necessary. Rather than meeting an animal, join with the womb space itself in a state of full reception. Imagine that you are in the darkness and must detect the environment by way of sensation and feeling. Become familiar with inner space by exploring. When you have completely shifted from the "mind's eye" to the inner sensory "eye" you will feel a stimulation of the third eye.

Sometimes it's easier to initiate sensing with your eyes <u>open</u>. Imagine that you can't look inside but you can feel around and it's 100 percent safe to do so. Pull the INbreath up from below and push the OUTbreath down into this space to anchor yourself. Remain here without trying to achieve anything. Invite the living consciousness of Love with a feeling of complete trust. Let yourself relax into this presence and rest there. There is no goal except to "be with."

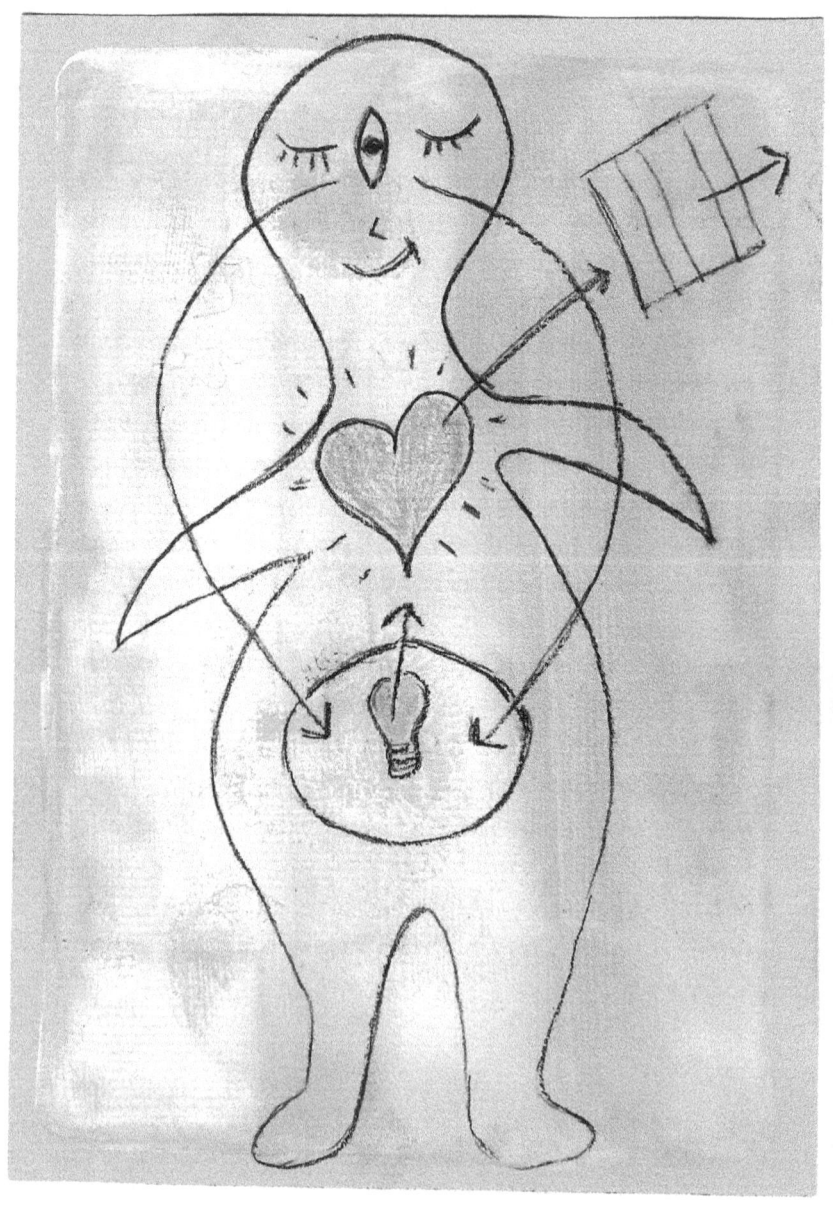

Resolving the separation.

After some time of practicing the previous exercises, you will have experienced feelings of relief, relaxation, safety and even bliss. These feelings pave the way for the heart wall to dissolve and for the heart to fully open.

If you move your attention up into the heart during any of those experiences, you will feel a soft but powerful expansion.

This doesn't mean that you will never feel pain in your heart again. In fact, you may feel pain more readily because you are no longer numbing yourself and this paves the way for deeper intimacy. There are many things that can and, in fact, should cause pain in our hearts. But the feeling of expansiveness is worth it. This is how justice comes about.

In those moments when you feel pain in your heart after the separation has been resolved, imagine that you are <u>taking a shower in it</u>. When you do this, you let the pain wash through you and you merge with it to cleanse. The pain needs to tell the story, but it doesn't need to stay and if you take a shower in it, it will pass through in a way that feels nourishing and real.

Meeting The Mother.

Meeting The Mother or Mother Web is not separate from Love or Truth or anything that occurs in the depths of the womb space, but the intention to join and communicate with this "entity" can take you deeper into a state of Bliss and will often result in some remarkable insights and epiphanies. Just like any telepathic communication it can be interactive in any way you choose. But on the first pass, in your premier encounter, it is best to expect nothing and ask for nothing. Simply be with. Nothing can harm you here. You are safe.

Initiate this meeting in the same manner as in the previous exercises.

Igniting the Inner Sun.

Entering the Love space repeatedly changes one's relationship to self and other. A feeling of satiation occurs that unhooks you from harmful habits and patterns. Integrity arises out of this, as well as the desire to serve. This is a ripening toward the relinquishment of the false self. The opportunity to overcome and surrender the "ego" will be presented. Our false identity obstructs the free flow of power through the solar plexus. When your sincere desire comes to meet this, you can make a request to surrender the false self, which will ignite the fire so that you become a purified instrument of Love. It takes time for the body to prepare for this, but as you continue to make the request, you will start to feel an opening and expansion of this area and a rushing of energy. Enjoy the "getting to know" part!

Directing Love.

When Love has been found, when the heart wall has dissolved, when the solar plexus is ignited (you will know), Love becomes a tool for transformation that can be directed via your focused awareness either in the Ether (telepathically) or in the physical. Your embodied presence will set to work on restructuring and reorganizing all that it comes into contact with. Your mission or destiny will become clear to take center stage in your life. For this, you need to be in the habit of remaining consciously embodied. If you visit the Love space every day, it will ultimately feel as if you never leave. And this is how you become Love *as a state of being.* This requires maintenance. Every night on your way to sleep and every morning upon waking, you have the opportunity to perform this maintenance! You will be inspired to direct Love. I can't tell you what form that will take, as this is unique to you. I can only ask you to trust this, trust Love, and trust yourself.

Below the level of thought,
where the bees live,
there is a pulse—
the rhythm of the one great heart.
In every moment that we
live below thought,
we are regenerated.

Donning the Ethereal Body.

The interior body of the physical is the ethereal body, which is infinitely immersed in the ethereal web. We exist within it no matter what. But when we are conscious of being OF it, another expansion occurs where The Knowing becomes our impeccable companion. This stimulates the third eye to "see" without interruption.

Imagine that beneath the outer skin of the physical is another suit that is ultralight. Your conscious engagement with this initiates a symbiotic relationship of mutual service. To be in the ethereal body is to notice it and feel it from within. The way to stimulate this is to imagine the inner skin of the ethereal body as your primary garb. At first this might make you feel dizzy as the weight of the physical drops away. The stimulation of the third eye feels like a heavy stone pressing down on the bridge of your nose and squeezing the space between your eyebrows. The more often you spend time here (eventually always), the more this pressure will unfurl as your inner sight is stirred. Soon the sensation of this eye will be ever present, and when it is not, you will notice and can re-engage, if needed. You will feel the lightness of your soul as the interior spaces are amplified. Your source of power will shift from the weightedness of the physical to the boundlessness of the ethereal.

The Celestial Body.

In a state of great purification and surrender, the ethereal body will disclose the celestial body, a constellation of consciousness that evolves the human form in devotion to humanity. At the point of uncompromising purification—the cleansing of the false self and the body through fasting and minimal consumption—we are presented with the option to merge with this body as a refined and numinous instrument that does not operate within the limitations of a singular identity.

It doesn't end here. The potential is great. We can call the formless into form to aid us in any mission we choose. We can set up councils and guardianships to assist or give watch over. We can guide others with communication that will enter their dreams or occur in flashes of knowing. We can commune telepathically to channel Love through modalities, such as craniosacral therapy, network chiropractic, homeopathy or those yet to be called into form. We can make direct requests or simply listen to become more intimate. We can communicate with other living systems via the ethereal network. I don't know the full potential, as I'm sure I have touched on only the tiniest bit of what is possible. This is why we need each other. This is why we will be working together to assert the vision that we are here to fulfill. Real change begins at the causal level. This is where we will meet and where the transfiguration of humanity begins.

Blessings to all who have come here to learn. I am honored to have the opportunity to share this small but essential piece of the vast remembrance.

RESOURCES TO SUPPORT EMBODIMENT

- Qi Gong and Tai Chi
- DVD: *Kundalini Yoga to Detox and Destress* with Maya Fiennes
- YogaLap YT channel: *Complete Breathwork/Pranayama* with Michael Bijker
- Pranic Living: *A lifestyle of reducing food intake by consuming "prana" (life force energy)*

SEPARATION: Predatory, Trauma-Driven, Authoritarian	UNION: Natural Governance, Egalitarianism, Sovereignty
Rules/Blame	Choice/Responsibility
Mind-centered	Home/Womb/Heart-centered
Intelllectualism, divided thinking	The Language of Nature, Holistic Thinking
"I decree" to control	"I join" to understand
Leaders and Followers	Collaborators
Fuels rebellion	Supports cooperation
Polarization	Unity
Merit-based	Intrinsic Value
External Motivation	Internal Motivation
Earning-focused	Service-focused
Ambition — distraction from self	Service — connection to self
Fosters narcissism	Fosters compassion
Competition (because worth is "earned")	Natural cooperation (because worth is inherent)
Ostracism	Inclusion
Seeking favoritism	Seeking connection
Special, greater than/less than	A part of, unique and integral
Rules	Inner Knowing
Force	Power
Violation of boundaries/soul displacement	Autonomous, sovereign, free
Insensitive to self and other	Sensitivity, awareness
Betrayal of self and other	Loyalty to self and other
Submission/supression	Expression, creation, growth
Isolation, despair, anxiety, depression	Connection, joy, feeling seen, heard, understood
TAKE	HONOR
Sympathy/pity	Empathy/compassion

SEPARATION: Predatory, Trauma-Driven, Authoritarian	UNION: Natural Governance, Egalitarianism, Sovereignty
Escape, suicide, addiction	Joy, union, communion
Dis-ease	Ease
Polarization	Balance
"Serve me or I will destroy you."	"You are powerful. My power is your power. We support one another in service to all."
Force demands service through submission	Power elicits service through support
Commodity/"get"	Inspiration
Manipulate, control	Communicate, seek understanding
Dependency	Empowerment
Disharmony, chaos, destruction	Harmony, order, clarity, vision
FEAR	LOVE
False power to few	Real power to all
Hoarding	Generosity
Poverty	Abundance
Hierarchy	Interconnected
Consumption	Communion
Emptiness	Sense of purpose integral to the whole
Deception	Trust
Power over	Power within
Powerless over impulses	Mastery over impulses
Beliefs/Ideologies from society	Guided from within
Good & Evil	Love & Truth
Projection/Reflection	Integration
Astral	Ethereal
False	True
Outer directed	Moving from the eternal womb

Outer to Inner
Outside Authority
- Routine
- Habit
- Programming
- Prescriptions for living, acting, behaving
    - what to eat
    - when to eat/sleep
    - how to live
- False/Fake
- Primarily trusting outer knowledge

Inner to Outer
Self-governance
- Flow
- Awareness
- Feeling/sensing
- Receiving
- Listening
    - to body
    - to self
- Healing
- Truth
- Authenticity
- Primarily trusting inner knowing

ABOUT THE AUTHOR

Susan Guran began a journey into the healing arts at the New England School of Homeopathy, where she was profoundly influenced by Dr. Paul Herscu's Cycles & Segments method—a framework that illuminates how patterns of expression in the mind and body holistically align with homeopathic remedies. This foundation sparked an enduring passion for exploring the subtle languages of healing.

As her practice deepened, Susan expanded beyond classical homeopathy into more intuitive realms, developing a sensitivity to the metaphorical language of the body and eventually, telepathic communication. This shift marked a turning point in her work, allowing her to engage with the unseen dimensions that shape our inner and collective experience.

Her professional path has included writing for *Equine Wellness Magazine* on the subject of homeopathy and working in equine-assisted therapies, which offered a window into non-verbal modes of connection. From 2010 to 2016, she maintained a classical homeopathy practice before evolving toward an integrative approach that unites intuitive perception, telepathic insight, and homeopathic principles. This book is the culmination of years of practice, study, and inner exploration. It offers a structured view of the unseen, inviting readers to expand their perceptual boundaries to engage in deeper transformative exchange and understanding.

www.ingramcontent.com/pod-product-compliance
Lightning Source LLC
Chambersburg PA
CBHW021012090426
CBR00007B/762